Dear M...

Enjoy!
Enjoy!
Aunt
Gloria
Brin

8/30/09

The Fine Art of Garnishing

jerry crowley

Art Director
Elaine L. Latham

Illustrated by
Hazel Croner

Photography by
John F. Latham
Plates #1, #4, #5
#6, #9, #10, #11

Publishers
Lieba Inc.
405 W. Franklin St.
Baltimore, Md. 21201

DEDICATION

To all cooks who take pleasure
in their creations . . . pride
in their accomplishments . . .
and time in their efforts.

Acknowledgements

There is nothing quite like the excitement of an idea. I am sure we have all experienced that inward surge of energy and excitement when we feel that we have "hit" upon something new or different. The seed of an idea creates an energy of its own and tends to torment its host until some action is taken to give it room to grow. So it was with me when I became excited about compiling and capturing the methods and techniques of the masters of garnishing.

The nurturing of an idea can sometimes be a long and tedious task filled with seemingly insurmountable obstacles if it were not for friends. The contribution of renewed excitement and knocking down of barriers to give my idea the room needed to grow and flourish came from these friends. Without them, the information here would still be somewhere in a file around my cluttered desk.

To Bea Schueck, my steadfast companion through this venture, who can smooth a phrase of English, correct misspelled words or add the proper punctuation where needed as easily as she can create a savory dish with a special flavor and quality which only she has. The tiresome research, collating and correcting which she has contributed to this finished product makes it possible for me to transmit my thoughts in a more easily understood fashion.

To Hazel Croner, my graphic illustrator, whose talented hands and attention to every detail has added so much to the finished product. My main objective was to produce a book of instructions which could be easily followed and understood in any kitchen. She has proven once again the age old adage, "one picture is worth a thousand words".

7

To John and Elaine Latham, who separately are the most energetic and creative people I know, and when teamed together, form a tornado of innovative thinking which is a marvel to watch. With their creative input, inspiration and encouragement it was possible for me to realize the full potential of the idea which excited me long ago. It is the "special" people who will not harbor negative thoughts such as "it will not work" or "it can't be done" that retain the ability to turn negative energy into a positive force which can accomplish the impossible. John and Elaine are two of these "special" people.

To the Chefs, both past and present, whose inspired creations and world of foie gras, subtle sauces and gloriously decorated dishes has set a goal for all enthusiastic cooks to reach. The artistic splendors produced by these culinary masters are the end result of painstaking and loving labor of many years of working among hot stoves, tasting soups, sampling sauces, and decorating many dishes before the final presentation.

Contents

9

RECIPES

Introduction

There is an old saying, and a very true one, it goes "that which is pleasing to the eyesight is also pleasing to the appetite". Of the multitude of books on food preparation and cooking I have encountered through my many years of studying culinary preparation and presentation, I have yet to find a book written with the sole purpose of instructing the reader, step by step, how to create professional complimentary garnishes and centerpieces. If such a book does exist that would solve only half of the problem; the other half being to find and round-up the tools needed to give the finished product a professional appearance. It was the unavailability of these tools and the information needed to use them properly which prompted me to put this kit together. With these tools and the instructions accompanying them you will be able to create masterful garnishes and centerpieces.

In American cooking we use the word 'garnish' to describe an edible ornament which is added to a main dish to make food much more satisfying to the eye and to the palate. In most cases we confine our garnishing to a few slices of tomatoes, thinly sliced, or some carrot curls and almost always a sprig of parsley. The French however take garnishing much more seriously and have well earned the reputation of being masters at it. To the French, garnishing is known as "garde manger" and is considered a fine art, as surely as paintings and sculptures. Reputations for fine food in many eating establishments are very much dependent upon the skills and talents of the garde manger chef.

In French cooking, garde manger means "food storage area"; the work which is done in this location has come to be also described by the term garde manger. The garde manger room was usually located next to the main kitchen in a cool, well-aired area with some type of food chilling facilities. It was important to have this room cool and away from the heat of the main kitchen because decorative designs could be worked out much more elaborately.

The methods and techniques of garde manger have been developed over centuries by Master Chefs and it is these talented and dedicated masters which have given garnishing a special place in culinary expertise. It is to these methods and techniques to which we dedicate this book. Some of the techniques are centuries old and cannot be changed while others have been carefully modernized so not to take anything away from the finished product. The collection of garnishing tools which accompany this book also hold the distinction of some being very old and others very modern.

Presenting food which is as pleasing to the eye as it is to the taste is the ultimate refinement of the cooking art. Even the most proficient chefs must master the art of garnishing because they realize that the appeal of food depends, to a great degree, upon its presentation. Garnishing gives food that finished look, but more than this it gives the cook a chance to extend 'creativeness'; to change a simple appetizer into an elegant dish, to enhance a main course into a conversation piece that will long be remembered. On many occasions the garnish around a well prepared and gratifying meal lingered in the memory of those who enjoyed that meal long after the main dish was forgotten.

The proper garnish to a main dish adds a new dimension to the food, and in a most dramatic way, informs the viewers that the cook's creative ability extends beyond just serving a savory dish. Those who feel that cooking is an enjoyable creative art, a skill which is mastered through trial and error, corrected mistakes and detailed instructions will have a pleasurable time matching their hand with the masters of garnishing.

No cook who honorably and proudly carries a reputation for being a "great cook" can hold that title undisputedly without having an understanding of garnishing. Garnishing is as important to food presentation as accessories are to a new outfit to achieve that well-dressed look.

Within the pages of this book you will find a way to master the creation of delightful and delicious garnishes and centerpieces. I will explain how to garnish from the simplest plate to the grandest buffet. Whether you are a Master Chef, professional cook, hostess, homemaker or a novice in the kitchen the value of learning the art of garnishing will be judged by the compliments returned to you for your displayed pride in setting an attractive table and will be well worth the efforts you put into learning this culinary art. Good luck and bon appétit!

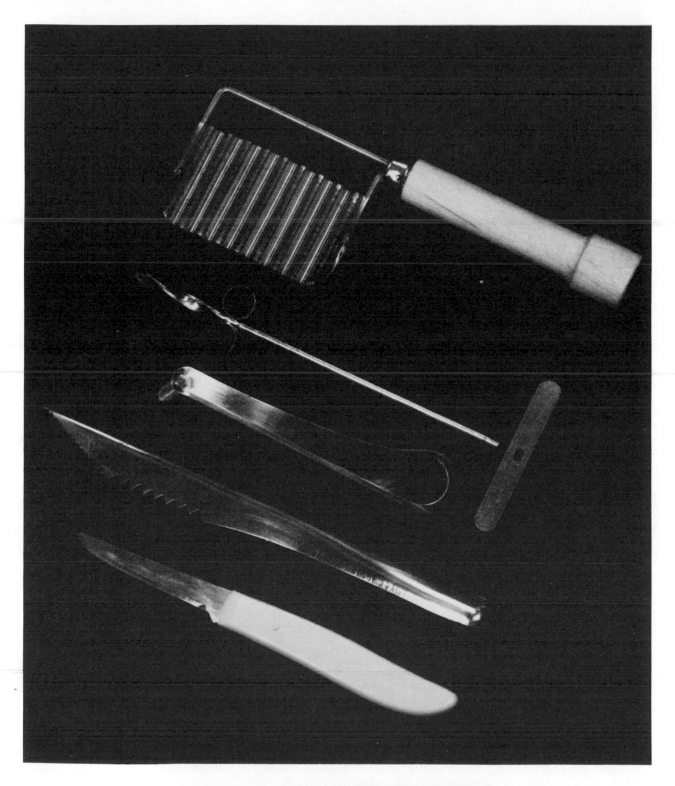

THE TOOLS OF THE TRADE

13

The Tools of the Trade

an introduction to the tools and equipment used for creating garnishes.

NOTE: If this book was purchased without tools and if you wish to acquire them, write to the publisher (see page 3)

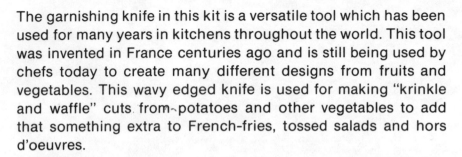

GARNISHING KNIFE

The garnishing knife in this kit is a versatile tool which has been used for many years in kitchens throughout the world. This tool was invented in France centuries ago and is still being used by chefs today to create many different designs from fruits and vegetables. This wavy edged knife is used for making "krinkle and waffle" cuts from potatoes and other vegetables to add that something extra to French-fries, tossed salads and hors d'oeuvres.

To make the scalloped design on vegetables, such as carrots, radishes, beets, potatoes, turnips and cucumbers, simply place the vegetable on a cutting surface and use the garnishing knife to slice the vegetable crosswise into ¼-inch slices. The garnishing knife works best on hard vegetables like carrots and beets if you parboil the vegetable before you cut it. The scalloped sliced vegetables can be mixed with cherry tomatoes, watercress and lettuce to create a tasty and eye-appealing salad.

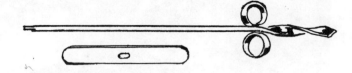

TWIN CURL CUTTER

The most exotic and unusual of the garnishing tools is the twin curl cutter. This tool is believed to have originated in Germany a very long time ago and is used to create vegetable and fruit curls of contrasting colors. It is also the handiest tool I know of to make delicious "stuffed vegetable surprise".

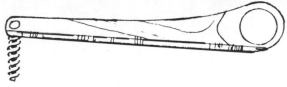

SPIRAL SLICER

The spiral slicer came out of American ingenuity and was invented sometime in the mid 1920's. This tool will transform your vegetables, such as carrots, beets, potatoes and radishes, into decorative coiled-up spiral ribbons These spiral ribbons are great attention getters when they are used to decorate cold relish platters, a buffet spread or used as a finishing touch to a main dish such as a turkey, ham, or leg of lamb.

FOOD DECORATOR TOOL

The food decorator tool with this kit was designed and invented In America and is a more modern garnishing tool. This tool is used to cut the time which was usually needed to create large centerpieces like watermelon baskets, viking ships and watermelon whales. This food decorator tool is an easy tool to use and will give your finished product that professional look. When making garnishes and centerpieces, you will find this tool indispensable in your kitchen. It can make small garnishes like radish roses and orange cartwheels quickly and easily in addition to adding the professional touch to your large centerpieces.

PARING KNIFE

The paring knife supplied with this garnishing kit has been custom made. It is designed to work as "an extension of your hand". It is important to be able to "feel" the food through the blade of the paring knife as you work in close. The most important function of a good paring knife is "control". A well designed paring knife should be comfortable to hold, sharp, and have a flexible blade. All these are important to give you control over the tip of the blade as well as the edge of the blade. The blade of this knife has been shortened to balance it for easy working and I am sure that this paring knife will become your favorite.

Do's and
Don'ts

The key word to remember when choosing a garnish is "complimentary". The garnish should compliment the food it is placed with, not only in color but in texture, size and taste. The garnish around a main dish should never mask or overpower the flavor of the food being presented. When carefully selected and well prepared, food will be attractive by virtue of its own natural goodness. A cook who wants the meal to look as good as it tastes and taste as good as it looks will learn to think color, size, texture and shape when choosing the best garnish for adding a new dimension to the food and to the whole meal.

Good food, well prepared, coupled with good design involving color, form and pleasing combinations all add up to a successfully garnished meal. Garnishes, as a rule, should not only be edible and attractive, they should also be tasty. As with most rules there are exceptions; when using a garnish around a main dish such as a rib roast, leg of lamb, ham, etc., it is permissible to use uncooked vegetables such as beets and turnips. Fresh flowers and fresh leaves are also in good taste when they are used properly. Plastic leaves and flowers will do little if anything at all, to enhance the appearance of food, so it is a good rule to stay away from anything artificial when garnishing.

Apple Garnishes

Probably the most universally enjoyed fruit is the apple which easily lends itself to the skill of the garnishing chef.

Choose a *fresh*, medium size, well rounded apple, the color you like best will do just fine. After the garnish is made, squeeze the juice of

1 lemon to 1 pint of water and pour this over the apple decoration to keep from turning brown.

Make sure you pick a *fresh* apple as many apples are held in cold storage. A fresh apple is easier to use and will last much longer.

Apple Bird

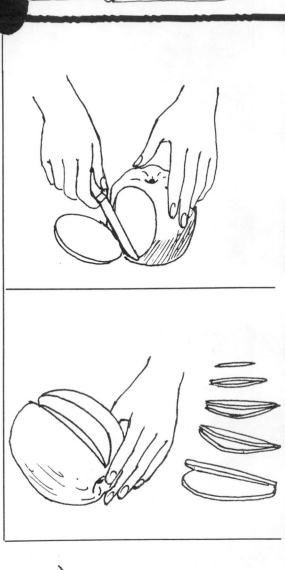

The apple bird is an ideal decoration for placing on a cheese, appetizer or hors d'oeuvre tray. This delightful garnish is relatively easy to make using the small paring knife. The juice of the apple aids in holding the birds' wings together, therefore it is important to use a fresh apple when making this garnish. To further enhance this decoration you can mix different color apples to alternate the wing colors.

1. Start the apple bird by slicing off a little less than one-third of the apple to create a flat surface. Save this piece to be used later for the neck and head.

2. Place the apple so it rests on it's flat surface. Using the small paring knife, cut a very small "V" wedge from the top of the apple. Set this wedge aside and cut another "V" wedge a little bit larger than the first. Continue cutting wedges (each a little larger than the other) until you have five or six of them. When working with a large apple, use a larger knife as the wedges become bigger.

3. After cutting the top wedges, turn the apple on its side and cut another series of wedges in the same way. After doing this, turn the apple to the other side and repeat the procedure. If it is going to be some time before the apple bird is to be displayed, place the wedges in a container of water to which the juice of one lemon has been added. Also wet the apple with the same solution.

Apple Bird

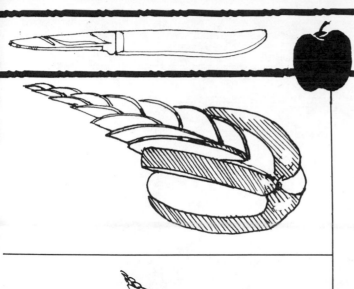

4. After all the "V" wedge slices have been cut, place the apple so it rests on the flat surface. Take the largest of the wedges and place it into the wedge-cut of the apple. Extend this wedge so that it protrudes slightly less than half-way towards the back of the apple. Place the next size smaller wedge into the larger wedge and continue extending the wedges.

5. Repeat the same procedure for the side wings. It is a good idea to put the "V" cut wedges back into the same part of the apple they came from.

6. To get the head and neck, slice a small strip from the piece of apple which was cut off to form the flat surface. Place this piece in the front groove of the apple. To help support the head and neck a toothpick can be used.

7. Once the apple bird is assembled, squeeze lemon juice over the entire bird to prevent it from turning brown. To perch the completed bird, cut a flat surface from a potato and with two toothpicks, set the bird on top of the potato.

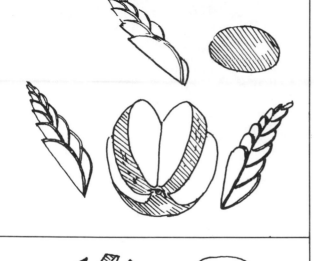

See Color Plate 6

Beet Garnishes

Beets — when used as garnishes — offer the cook a chance to extend creativity.

The beet rose is the most sophisticated and elegant of the vegetable garnishes. When mixed with greens or other vegetable flowers, it can be used to create beautiful centerpieces for any table or as a garnish on a bed of fresh parsley around the base of any meat, game or poultry platter. Use your imagination to create many different designs.

It is also the most difficult to make and is to be used as a garnish for visual purposes only. Since it is carved from the uncooked vegetable it is not meant to be eaten.

ROSE CENTERPIECE

To make a beautiful centerpiece for your table begin by shaping a small piece of chicken wire into a dome. Fill the spaces of the chicken wire by poking fresh parsley or watercress through these openings to create a mound of greenery. Arrange the vegetable flowers around this mound of greenery by securing them to the chicken wire with toothpicks.

Beet Carved Rose

The beet carved rose is the most elegant of the vegetable flowers. This rose also takes the most practice because it is hand carved from the raw vegetable. Before attempting to make the rose from the beet or turnip you should practice carving this flower from a potato. The potato is much easier to work with and any mistakes can be turned into sliced or mashed potatoes and nothing will be wasted.

1. To start the rose, select a well rounded beet and cut the vegetable in half. Hold one of the halves in one hand and with the other hand, use the small knife and cut a petal just below the flat surface of the beet.

Cut these petals as if you were going to peel the vegetable, cutting close to, but not all the way through the base. Try to keep the petals as thin and rounded as possible.

2. Place the point of the knife between any of the two petals you have cut around the outside of the beet and cut out a thin ring from the inside of the vegetable.

3. Cut this ring in a continuous strip as you would do when peeling an apple.

4. After you have completed the second step it is just a matter of repeating these two steps, working towards the center of the vegetable. After removing the first ring from inside the first row of petals, start cutting the second row of petals, cutting them the same way as the first row was made. Each row of petals should be cut so they alternate. This is done by cutting the inside petal between the two outside petals of the row you just finished.

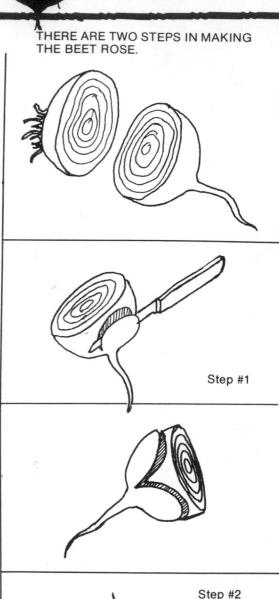

THERE ARE TWO STEPS IN MAKING THE BEET ROSE.

Step #1

Step #2

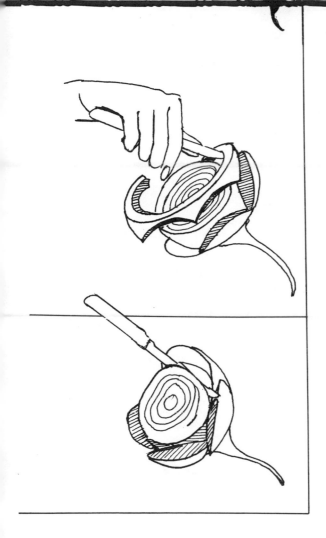

5. You will notice, as the flower progresses, that the rings you have cut out will get smaller and smaller until you have reached the center, or core, of the vegetable. The more rows of petals you can carve out the more striking and life like the rose will look.

It is just a matter of practice before you can produce beautiful vegetable roses. Once you have mastered the carved rose, you are only restricted by your imagination as to the many centerpieces and garnishes you can create with them. For an elegant centerpiece on a buffet table, carve these roses from both red beets and white turnips and arrange them on a background of fresh parsley or watercress to create a beautiful bouquet of red and white roses.

NOTE: The carved beet roses can be made ahead (in the summer when beets are in season and not expensive) and frozen until needed. To freeze the carved beet roses they must be placed in a container of water and completely submerged before freezing.

To two-tone or accent the turnip rose, cut off a thin slice of beet and brush it across the tips of the turnip flower. This will give the turnip rose a new look.

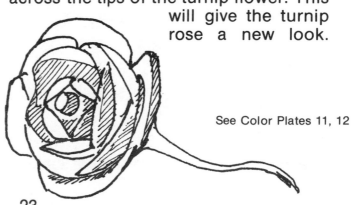

See Color Plates 11, 12

Beet Strip Rose

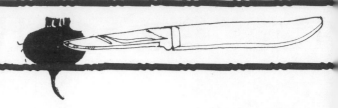

Another variation of the beet roses, and one which is very attractive when set on parsley and used to garnish a meat, fish or poultry platter, is the beet strip rose.

1. To make this vegetable flower, select a medium-sized beet and peel the outside skin. Use a vegetable peeler and pare a long continuous strip around the outside of the vegetable.

Peel the vegetable as you would an apple to get the long thin strip. Try to get the strips at least 3 to 4 inches long.

2. After you have 2 or 3 of these long strips, place them in salt water solution (1 tablespoon salt, 1 quart water) for 5 minutes.

3. Use the longest beet strip and wrap it into a loose coil. Take the shortest of the strips and roll it tightly. Place this tightly rolled strip into the center of the first coiled strip to form the rose. Shape the flower to acquire a full-blooming rose.

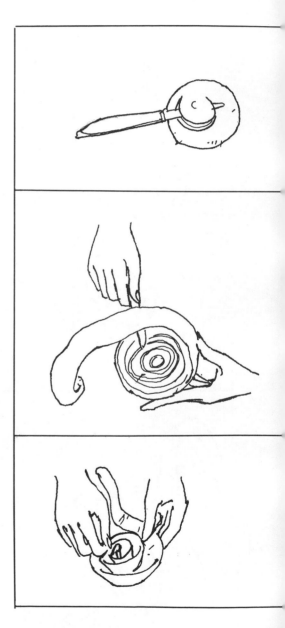

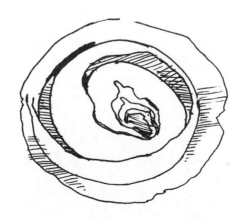

Beet Sliced Rose

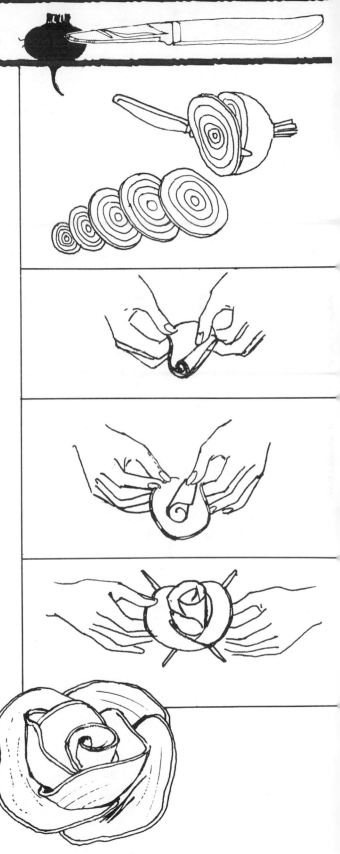

1. Wash and peel a medium-sized, well rounded beet. Use a vegetable slicer or a sharp knife and cut 5 or 6 paper-thin slices from the beet. Start cutting these slices from the root end of the vegetable.

Place the slices into a solution of salt water (1 tablespoon salt, 1 quart water) for about 5 minutes to soften the petals.

2. Use the smallest slice and roll it up tightly.

3. Take the next smallest slice and wrap it around the first rolled slice. From here on wrap each petal in the opposite direction as they are added to the flower.

4. Roll additional slices around each other, using the larger slices for the outside petals.

Secure the rolled slices with toothpicks. Use 2 or 3 toothpicks at the base of the rolled petals.

After securing the rolled pedals with the toothpicks, gently fold down the outside petals and shape the rose.

When the rose is fully shaped, place it in ice water for 5 minutes to set the shape.

NOTE: These beet sliced roses can be frozen for later use if placed in a container of water. The flowers must be completely under water when freezing.

Beet Asters

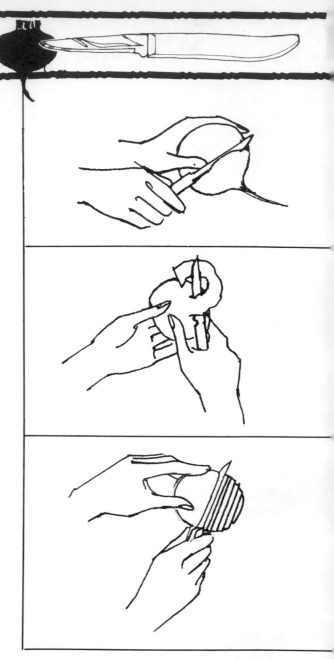

The beet aster is very easy to make and adds another variety of vegetable flower for creating centerpieces and garnishes for a platter of cold meat, relish tray or mixed vegetable flower centerpiece for buffet spreads.

1. To make the beet aster, select a well-rounded, medium-sized beet and cut off the top and root end of the vegetable to create a flat surface.

2. Peel the beet completely.

3. With the knife, make a series of parallel cuts. Start these cuts from the stem end and slice all the way to, but not through, the root end of the vegetable. Stop the cut about ¼-inch from the root end. Cut the slices as close together as possible.

4. When you have completed this series of cuts, give the beet a quarter turn and cut a second set of parallel cuts across the first cuts forming right angles.

5. Chill the vegetable in ice water and when ready to use, gently spread the petals to form the aster.

NOTE: To make a mixed bouquet of asters, use white turnips and follow the same instructions for making the beet asters. The turnip asters can be colored by placing a few drops of vegetable food coloring in the ice water to tint the flowers in a variety of colors.

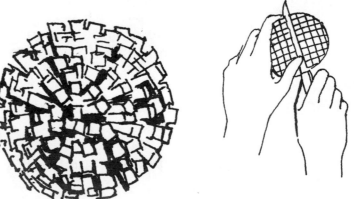

Beet Spirals

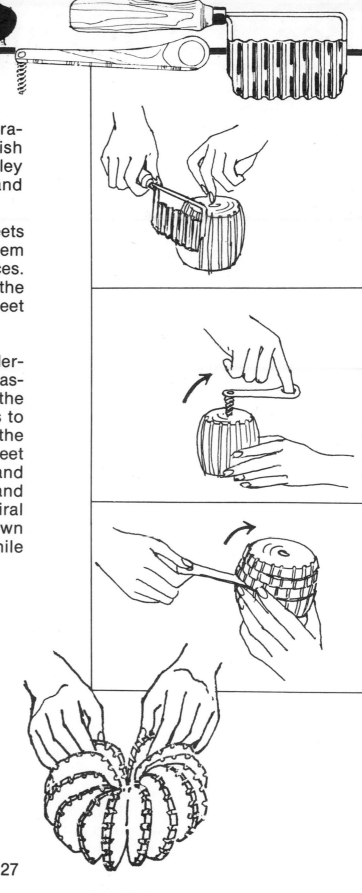

The beet spiral makes an impressive decoration when used as a centerpiece for a relish tray or when they are placed on fresh parsley and set at each corner of a meat entre and topped with a radish rose.

1. To make the beet spiral, select beets which are oval in shape. Cut the stem and root ends to create flat surfaces. Use the garnishing knife around the outside of the vegetable to give the beet a ripple edge.

2. Use the spiral slicer and with a moderate pressure, push the point of the plastic screw into the core, or center, of the beet. Give the vegetable a few turns to allow the screw to catch hold. Once the screw has grabbed hold, place the beet securely in your left hand (right hand if left handed) and with the other hand turn the spiral slicer. Allow the spiral slicer to wind into the beet at its own pace, do not apply pressure while turning.

3. After the spiral slicer has sliced through about half way, hold the blade of the slicer steady and turn the beet into the blade. This way you will be able to slice completely through the beet.

4. Wash the sliced beet under warm water to remove the beet juice and interlock the two ends of the beet spiral to form the decoration. Place a radish rose on top of the beet spiral for a finishing touch.

27

Beet Candy Cane

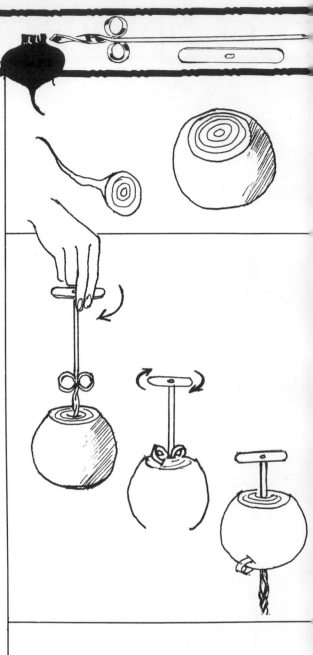

The twin curl cutter in the garnishing kit is a garnishing tool used to create vegetable and fruit curls of contrasting colors. You can make garnishes from carrots, beets, potatoes and turnips by intertwining the different vegetables together to create eye-appealing and appetizing garnishes for relish trays, salads and holiday occasions. The candy cane beet never fails to get a delightful response at Christmas time and it will mystify those who do not know how they are made.

1. To make the beet candy cane garnish, select a large beet and cut the stem and root off to create a flat surface.

2. Attach the "T" handle to the top of the double ringed shaft. Insert the point of the tool into the center of the vegetable. Use a slight pressure and turn the tool clockwise into the center of the beet until the double rings start to cut through the vegetable. Continue using a slight pressure while turning the tool clockwise until the rings cut all the way through the vegetable and come out the bottom end of the beet. After the tool is completely through, remove the "T" handle and slide the twin curl cutter out of the vegetable.

3. TURN, do not pull, the cut portion from the center of the beet. Once you have turned the curls from the beet, they can be easily separated by gently turning each curl in the opposite direction of each other. This will produce two beet curls.

4. Repeat the same procedure on a turnip to get the white curls. Take one beet curl and one turnip curl and twist them into each other to make candy

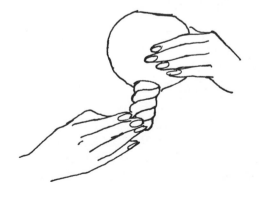

28

Beets Stuffed

Beet Candy Cane...

    cane garnishes. When ready to serve, simmer these vegetable candy canes in lightly salted water for 10 minutes and serve.

    After using the twin curl cutter on beets or turnips, the hollowed vegetable can be filled with seasoned meats or cheese to create a novel and delicious filled vegetable.

STUFFED BEETS

5. Cook the hollowed out beets in lightly salted water until tender. Cool and remove the skins. Heat oven to 350°F (moderate). Mix the cheese, bread crumbs, sour cream, pickle relish and seasonings. Stuff this mixture into the hollowed out centers of the beets and place them on a shallow greased baking dish. Brush with butter and bake uncovered in 350°F oven for 15 to 20 minutes. Melt the butter and mix with the white wine and baste occasionally to keep moist. Serves 6.

BEET CUPS

Beet or turnip cups are an appetizing way to present cooked vegetables and also offer an easy way to portion-control servings for a buffet.

To make this easy and useful garnish, select large sized beets and wash in cold water. Cut off the stem and root ends creating a flat surface. Cook the whole vegetable in lightly salted water until tender. After cooked and cooled, use a small sharp knife and carefully cut out the centers, or cores, of the beets leaving about ½-inch of the shell to form the vegetable cups. When ready to serve, fill the cups with cooked vegetables such as green peas, spinach, carrots or mashed potatoes. Finish by garnishing with a sprig of fresh parsley.

STUFFED BEETS
- 6 large beets
- 6 tablespoons grated sharp cheese
- 2 tablespoons bread crumbs
- 2 tablespoons sour cream
- 1 tablespoon pickle relish
- ½ teaspoon salt
- ¼ teaspoon pepper
- ¼ cup butter
- ¼ cup white wine

See Color Plate 10

Carrot Garnishes

Another of the most common of garnishes, and one which is easy to work with, is the carrot. Raw carrot garnishes offer that little bit of crunch needed to compliment main dishes that have a soft texture such as a meat-loaf, fish dinners and most casseroles. Carrot garnishes also offer an appealing color contrast to foods because the carrot is one of the few vegetables available throughout the year that gives us the orange color needed to contrast the green leafy salads and main dishes. People who would not normally eat raw carrots will not hesitate to munch on a carrot garnish if it is presented in the right way.

When selecting carrots, for either cooking or garnishing, choose medium-sized ones with the tops still attached and ones with good color. To test for freshness break off a small piece of the root end. If a sharp snap is heard then you can be sure that the vegetable is fresh.

Carrots, once sliced, can be formed into different shapes and made to hold that shape by keeping them in cold water. There are quite a variety of garnishes which can be made with the carrot that are tempting to the eye, easy to eat and fun to make.

Carrot Sticks

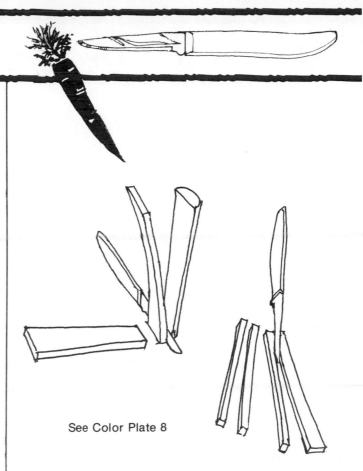

1. Carrot sticks are a very popular vegetable in a relish tray and offer a pleasing contrast in color and crunch when mixed with other vegetables. To make the carrot sticks, select a fat, squatty carrot. Cut off about ½-inch of the root end and stem end. Wash the vegetable in cold water. With a small knife cut long strips (about ¼-inch thick) the full length of the carrot. Keep the cuts as even and straight as possible.

2. Cutting the vegetable this way should produce wide strips which are then laid flat to be sliced again into 4-inch strips. Trim each carrot stick to a length of about 3-inches. If the carrot sticks are placed in ice water they will curl around to form half circles. These half circles can be arranged so that they form an orange vegetable ring in a relish tray for holding black and green olives.

See Color Plate 8

See Color Plate 7

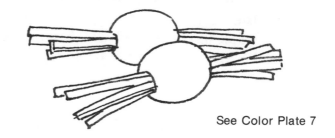

See Color Plate 7

OLIVE DUMB-BELLS

For another attractive munchie on a sandwich plate or relish tray you can use the carrot sticks to make edible dumb-bells by simply putting a pitted olive on each end of the carrot stick. You can also put a small amount of cream cheese into the pitted olive to hold the carrot stick securely.

CARROT BUNDLES

Another variation of the carrot and olive combination is the carrot bundle. These are made by threading a few carrot sticks through a pitted black or green olive to form a vegetable bundle which is temptingly easy to munch on. The carrot bundle also adds a nice garnish to individual sandwich plates.

Carrot Twists

The secret to making this delightful garnish is soaking them in a salt water solution. The carrot twist has much eye-appeal when used in a salad or when placed as a garnish for a sandwich plate.

1. To make this garnish, cut off the tip end of a fat carrot.

2. Follow the same procedure for making the carrot curl but instead of curling the strip, cut it into 3-inch lengths.

3. Cut a 1-inch slot down the center of each 3-inch strip.

Soak these strips in the salt water solution for 15 minutes. This will soften the strips enough to work with.

4. Insert one end of the strip through the center slot and gently pull it straight back to form the twist. Soak the finished twists in ice water to set the shape.

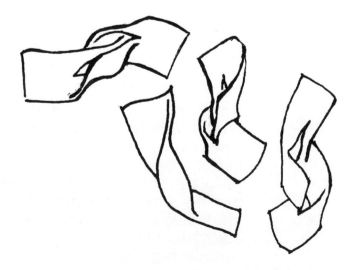

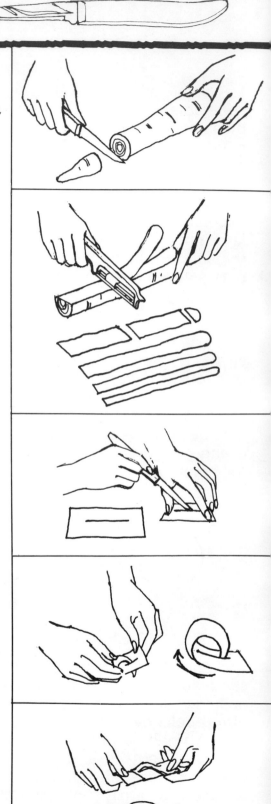

32

Carrot Wheels

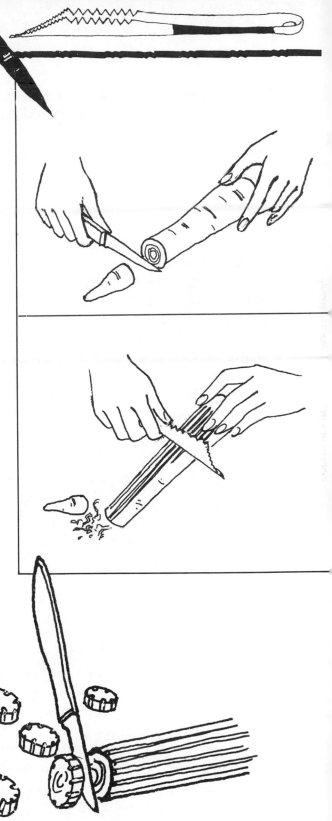

Carrot garnishes also offer an appealing color contrast to foods because the carrot is one of the few vegetables available throughout the year that gives us the orange color needed to contrast the green leafy salads and main dishes. People who would not normally eat raw carrots will not hesitate to munch on a carrot garnish if it is presented in the right way.

1. The carrot cartwheels, when used in a salad or soup, add that little "something extra". To make cartwheels, wash and cut off about ½-inch of the carrot tip.

2. Use the decorator tool and scrape the outside length of the carrot using a downward stroke only. This is known as 'scoring' the vegetable. The downward scrape will create small ridges all around the outside of the carrot.

After scoring the vegetable, slice the carrot crosswise and you will get small carrot slices with a geared or cartwheel edge. Mix these slices into a tossed salad or use them in your favorite soup.

Carrot Curls

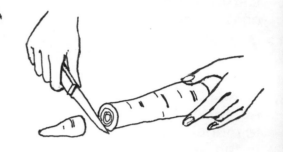

1. It is easiest to make the carrot curl when the vegetable is allowed to reach room temperature. To make the carrot curls, select a fat, uniformly tapered carrot and wash in cold water. Cut about ½-inch off the tip, or root end, of the vegetable.

2. Use a vegetable peeling knife (the swivel vegetable peelers work best) and peel a strip the full length of the carrot. Create a flat side on the carrot to prevent it from rolling around when making the strips needed for the carrot curls. Hold the carrot steady in one hand, place the peeler flat against the top rounded side of the carrot and with an even pressure and quick stroke, run the peeler down the full length of the carrot, pushing the peeler away from you.

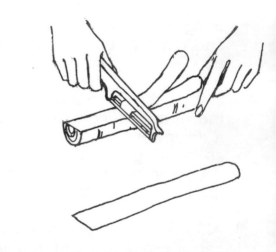

3. Continue with the peeler. Roll up the wide strips with your fingers and secure the curled strips by placing a toothpick through the rolled strip. Drop these rolled carrot curls into ice water and refrigerate for several hours to set the curl. Remove the toothpick before serving.

CARROT ZIGZAGS:
Thread the carrot strips onto a toothpick in a zigzag style. Place the zigzag strips into ice water and refrigerate for several hours. Remove the toothpick before serving.

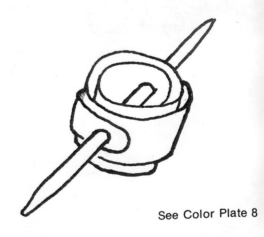

See Color Plate 8

34

Carrot Spiral

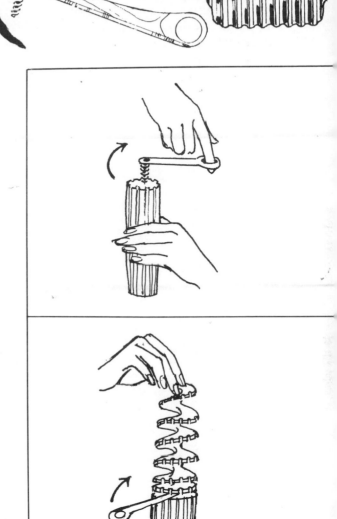

1. To make the carrot spiral, score the vegetable and use the Spiral Slicer. Select a fat, squatty carrot and wash it in warm water to bring to room temperature. Cut about ½-inch off the stem end of the vegetable, creating a flat surface. Push the point of the plastic screw into the center, or core, of the carrot. Give the carrot a few turns to allow the screw to catch hold.

2. As you rotate the tool the blade will come down slowly to meet the vegetable. Do not apply any downward pressure on the tool. Allow the spiral to wind into the vegetable at its own pace.

3. Hold the vegetable straight up and down in one hand and rotate the Spiral Slicer with the other. After you have sliced through 3- or 4-inches, break off that portion of the carrot which has been sliced.

4. As a decorative garnish interlock, or overlap, the two ends of the vegetable. This will form a rounded bracelet-shaped garnish. Tack the ends with a toothpick and chill in ice water for 10 minutes to set the shape. This garnish makes an impressive decoration when used as a centerpiece for a relish tray or when it is placed on fresh parsley and set at each corner of a meat entré. Remove toothpick when ready to use.

NOTE: To remove the Spiral Slicer from the uncut portion of the vegetable, reverse the rotation going counter-clockwise and the screw of the tool will back itself out without force.

See Color Plate 8

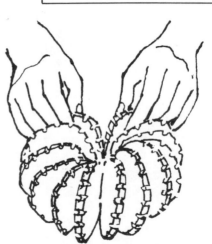

Celery Garnishes

Celery, a tasteful vegetable whether prepared raw or cooked, has a very interesting background.

It was cultured to its present state from a wild white flower herb found in Europe and Asia. Celery was originally grown as a medicinal plant until the 17th Century.

It is a most difficult plant to grow but certainly worth the rewards when enjoyed in soup or stew or turkey stuffing. Celery is especially rewarding when prepared as a tempting and enjoyable garnish as shown on the following pages.

Celery Flutes

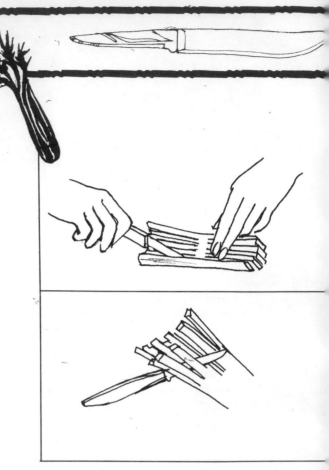

1. Clean pieces of celery and cut the stalks into 3-inch lengths. Using the inner stalks to make the flute will make it much more tender and less stringy. Hold the 3-inch stalk in one hand and with the other hand use a small knife and cut short slices, keeping them close together and as straight as possible.

2. Make cuts from the outside end of the stalk toward the middle. Cut these slices about 1-inch deep cutting from the end to, but not through, the middle.

3. When finished, turn the stalk around and do the other end in the same way. Chill in ice water and refrigerate until the strips curl. When ready to serve place these celery flutes on a relish tray along with carrot curls, pickle fans or stuffed pickles, radish roses, cucumber slices and black and spanish olives.

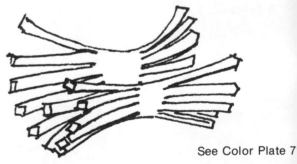

See Color Plate 7

CELERY HEARTS:

1. The yellow-white center part of the celery is called the heart and this part of the vegetable is considered by many people to be a real delicacy. Remove the heart from the inside of the stalk of celery. Do not remove any of the small leaves. Wash in cold water and cut off the hard part of the base. When ready to serve, place these hearts on top of a tossed salad or on a relish tray mixed with other appetizing garnishes.

Celery Stuffed

Celery is always a pleasing garnish and it is another of the vegetable garnishes which add an appetizing crunch to any meal. Celery can be used by itself or the stalks can be filled with any number of savory mixtures such as cream cheese, smoke-flavored cheese, deviled ham or chopped liver. If a cheese mixture is used, it should be softened with a little milk to which you can add spices, chopped chives, onions or parsley. Any of the celery garnishes will add contrast and substance when used as an appetizer or with salad and sandwich plates. If you are going to use the celery hearts and would like to do something nice with the outside stalks, then stuffing them is the answer.

1. Wash and trim the leaves and bottom part of the stalks.

2. Fill the trimmed stalks with any cheese spread which has been softened with a little milk. Add spices, chopped onions, chives or parsley to the softened mixture and whip until smooth and fluffy. Fill the inside of the stalks with this cheese mixture.

3. Take the filled stalks and place them together, cheese to cheese, then tie the stalks together with a little string and refrigerate.

4. When ready to serve, remove the string and cut the stalks crosswise into bite size slices. Place these filled slices on a relish tray or alongside a sandwich.

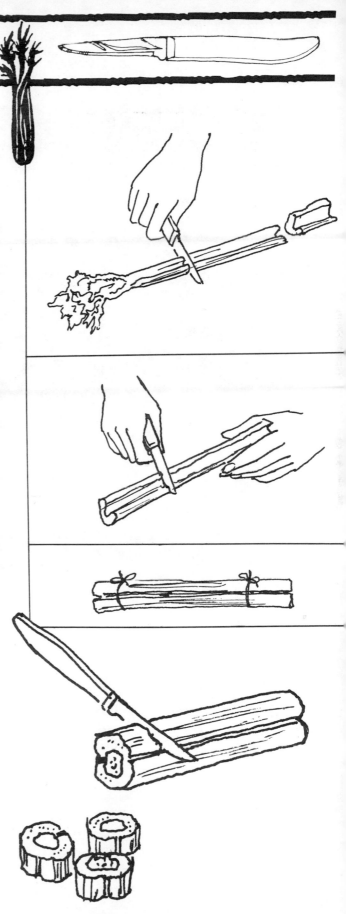

40

Cucumber Garnishes

Cucumbers and pickles, especially sweet gherkins, do make eye appealing and mouth watering garnishes. Whenever appetizers are served which consist of bread or crackers then some type of cucumber or pickle garnish should be used.

Many people do not know that a gherkin is a small undeveloped but genuine cucumber. When the cucumber has grown 2 to 3-inches long, it is picked and placed in a barrel filled with a salt or sweet brine mixture. The pickle, of course, is a cucumber which has been allowed to grow to its full maturity before being picked and placed in the brine mixture to be pickled.

A pickle garnish adds a decorative touch, perks up the taste buds and adds a delightful crunch to soft textured foods. Pickle or cucumber garnishes will enhance the appearance and taste of sandwich or salad plates, macaroni, potato or chefs salads. Pickle and cucumber garnishes are easy to make and will convey the message that the food has been prepared and served with care.

Cucumber Flower

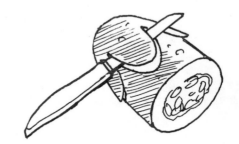

The cucumber flower is not only a pleasing garnish but also one that is easy to make.

1. Select a well-rounded cucumber and cut 2-inch pieces from each end of the vegetable. Cut the outside skin into scallop shapes to form the petals.

2. Scoop out the center pulp of each piece with either a melon baller or a small spoon.

Place the scalloped pieces into ice water for 15 minutes to allow the petals to open.

3. When the cucumber flower is ready to serve, remove them from the ice water and fill the centers with softened cream cheese, smoke flavored cheese, ham spread, shredded carrots or cooked green peas. These vegetable flowers can also be used to hold tartar sauce for fish dinners, mayonnaise or mustard for sandwich plates.

Cucumber Palm

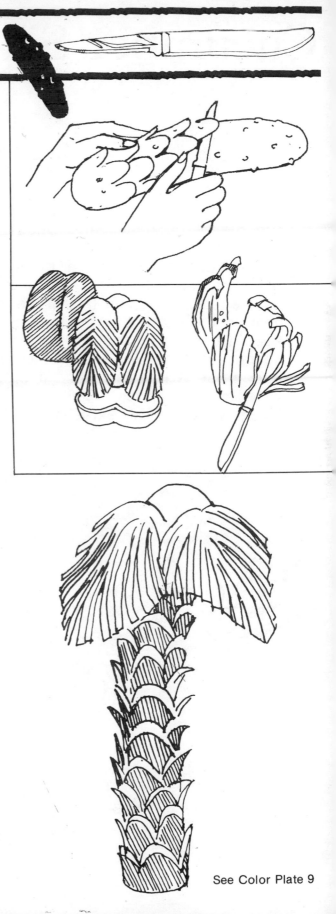

The cucumber palm tree is an ideal center-piece for a Luau Spread. The trunk of the palm tree can be made from either a cucumber, zucchini or carrot. Each of these vegetables will easily spread open to resemble the bark of the palm tree. The palm tree should be made at least 1 day ahead to give the leaves and trunk enough time to spread and curl.

1. To make the trunk of the tree use the paring knife and cut small round gashes into the skin of the vegetable. Start at the bottom of the vegetable and continue cutting the gashes around and up to the top end. Alternate the cuts to give the trunk a more realistic look.

2. After all the cuts have been made, cut one end of the vegetable to create a flat surface so the trunk can stand up. Place the finished trunk into ice water and let stand at least 1 day to open. For the leaves of the palm tree, use a green bell pepper. Select a pepper which has 3 "rounds" on the top. Cut these rounds into oval shapes but be careful not to cut into the top section which holds the rounds together. Make a series of diagonal cuts, close together, into but not all the way to the center of each oval leaf.

3. When ready to assemble the palm tree, slice a potato in half lengthwise. Place one half of the potato with the flat side down. Use 2 or 3 toothpicks and push them into the potato at the spot the palm tree is going to be placed. Set the flat end of the cucumber trunk down onto the protruding toothpicks. Place the pepper leaves on top of the trunk and secure with another toothpick.

43

See Color Plate 9

Cucumber Scored

For an added fancy touch to cucumber slices, select a medium-sized cucumber and trim one end to create a flat surface. With the Food Decorator tool, run the #1 opening (Strip Cutter) of the tool down the length of the un-peeled cucumber. Use a moderate pressure to cut through the skin of the vegetable. Repeat this procedure around the outside of the cucumber, keeping the peeled strips as evenly spaced as possible. After the scored cucumber is finished, slice it cross-wise into thin slices. These scored slices will add a little extra touch when used in a tossed salad or on a relish tray.

CUCUMBER TWISTS

Follow the instructions for the scored cucumber. Cut the scored vegetable into slices about ¼-inch thick.

1. With the blade of a small peeler knife, make a cut from the center, or middle, of the scored cucumber slice to the outside edge.

2. Gently twist the cut slice in opposite directions to form an "S" shaped twist. Hold this shape in place with a toothpick and refrigerate in ice water to set shape. Remove the toothpick before serving.

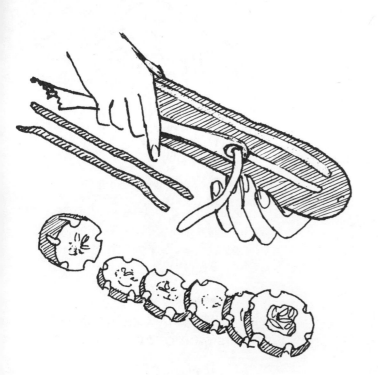

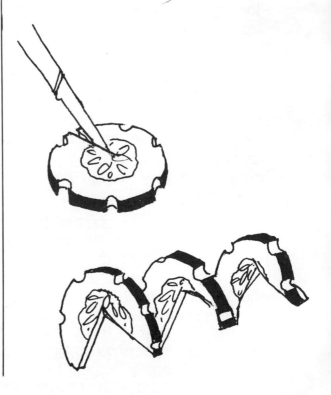

Cucumber Stuffed

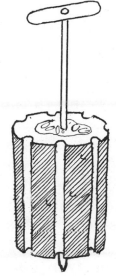

Another interesting and delicious garnish to make from the cucumber is the stuffed cucumber relish. Follow the same procedure of hollowing out the vegetable using the twin curl cutter in the same fashion as described under cucumber chains.

Do not slice the hollowed vegetable but instead choose one of the recipes below and pack the cucumber shell tightly with the mixture. After filling the shell, refrigerate it until ready to use. When ready to serve, slice the stuffed cucumber into ¼-inch pieces. Use these stuffed slices in a relish, appetizer or sandwich tray.

SOFTENED CREAM CHEESE MIX

Soften cream cheese with a small amount of milk or cream and whip until a smooth consistency is obtained. Add pickle relish (drained), chopped chives or minced onions to the cream cheese mixture. Mix until well blended.

ROQUEFORT CHEESE MIX

Mix together ½ pound of Roquefort cheese, ½ pound butter, and the yolks of 4 hard cooked eggs to a fine paste. Stuff cucumber and refrigerate until ready to use. After slicing the stuffed cucumber, sprinkle the slices with paprika.

SALMON CREAM FILLING

Blend together 6 ounces smoked salmon (shredded) with 3 ounces sour cream. Add ½ cup finely chopped green onion, 1 teaspoon dried dill, and dash of garlic powder. Fill the hollowed cucumber shell with this salmon mixture and refrigerate until ready to use.

Cucumber Chain

1. The cucumber chain garnish presents a most pleasing decoration, not to mention a tasty one, when used to encircle a fish entré or when run around the outside of an appetizer and relish tray. Cut both ends of a medium-size cucumber to create flat surfaces. With the Food Decorator tool, run the #1 opening (Strip Cutter) of the tool down the length of the unpeeled cucumber.
(see Cucumber Scored p. 44)

2. Use the twin curl cutter to hollow out the center of the vegetable (see Beet Candy Cane p. 28). Since the cucumber has a soft center, the twin curl cutter will not produce solid curls but this tool still does a neat job of hollowing out the vegetable.

3. After you have hollowed the cucumber, cut it into ¼-inch thick slices. Spread the cucumber slices out and make a small cut from the center of the slice to the outside. Do this to every other cucumber slice and link the slices together to form a chain.

See Color Plate 10

Cucumber Boat

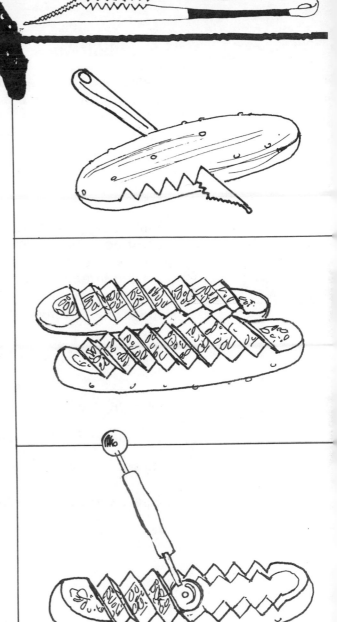

FOR COLD SAUCES

Cucumber boats add an appealing touch to any buffet spread or dinner plate. This vegetable boat is very attractive and effective when you need a container to hold mustard, mayonnaise, sour cream or any other cold sauce. If you are going to use the cucumber boats in this way, follow the instructions below but do not peel or cook the vegetable.

FOR HOT VEGETABLES

1. To make the vegetable boat, select a medium-size cucumber and peel the outside skin. Make a cut down the vegetable to form a flat side. Set the vegetable on the flat side and make a cut 1-inch in from each end of the cucumber. Start at the end of the cucumber with the decorator tool and push the point of the tool through the middle of the vegetable. This will create a "V" Cut through the cucumber. Make another cut in the same way right next to the first cut. Continue making these cuts to each other being sure to connect each new cut.

2. Separate the two halves and with a small spoon or melon baller remove the seeds and pulp of the cucumber to form the boat.

3. After the boat is made, cook it in lightly salted water just long enough to soften the shell. When ready to serve, fill the cucumber boat with cooked vegetables such as creamed carrots, peas, cooked beets, lima beans or spinach and serve as a vegetable side dish.

Eggplant Vase

Select a uniform eggplant of good color. Cut a flat surface on both ends. Slice a turnip into ⅛" slices. Using the knife point, cut out 4 or 5 petal designs from the turnip slices. Attach these flowers on the eggplant vase using toothpicks. Leave a small portion of the toothpick protruding from the turnip flower. From the tapered end of a carrot, cut small thin slices and place on the end of the toothpick for the flower center.

Fill your eggplant vase with a lovely vegetable flower arrangement by using toothpicks for low flower arrangements and long green floral sticks to create high flower arrangements. These long sticks can be hidden easily by cutting scallion tops the length of the sticks and slipping them over the sticks before attaching the vegetable flowers.

There are a variety of greens available to accent your arrangement. For some vegetable suggestions see page 59.

See page 90 for Scallion Flowers

See page 58 for Cucumber Leaf

See page 94 for Tomato Stripe Rose

See page 89 for Radish Rose

See page 79 for Pepper Flower

In the next 8 pages you will see a visual delight that will stun the imagination. We hope you enjoy it and that it will stimulate you in pursuing the "Fine Art of Garnishing".

Eggplant Bouquet

Color Plate 1

Watermelon Whale

Color Plate 2

50

Watermelon Basket   Color Plate 3

51

Apple Birds On The Wing   Color Plate 6

Tomato Surprise   Color Plate 7

Creative Relish Tray

Color Plate 8

Paradise Island   Color Plate 9

Luncheon Delight   Color Plate 10

Roses From the Vegetable Garden   Color Plate 11

Holiday Feast

Color Plate 12

Dear Cuisineer:

Now that you've seen it, all the real fun begins. It begins now, for dinner tonight — a bed of lettuce leaves with cottage cheese and a tomato rose on top then dress up with a few radish roses. You'll have fun doing it and enjoy the lovely compliments you'll receive.

Your family and friends will be proud of the new "artist" in the family.

When you have company, they will be surprised and delighted at your garnishing skills and no doubt you'll be the center of their conversation for a long time afterward.

Drop me a line with your name and address and as I develop new designs I will be happy to share them with you and naturally I would like to see yours.

Garnishingly yours,

Chef Jerry

Cucumber Leaves

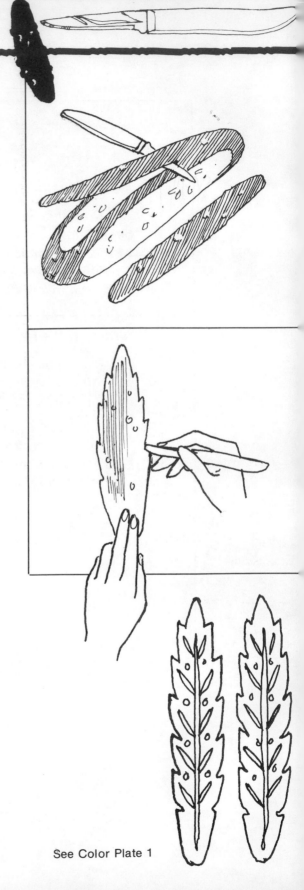

A vegetable flower centerpiece or garnish is never complete without the accent of greenery. The green foliage around, or in a vegetable flower arrangement adds depth to color, authenticity to design and interest to the arrangement.

The most common greenery used when garnishing is parsley which is available in the markets throughout most of the year. Parsley is an ideal foliage to use when creating garnishes which will lay flat around a meat entré or in the center of a relish tray.

If you are making a high vegetable flower centerpiece such as the eggplant vase arrangement (see Color Plate #1 page 49) then greenery which will stand and act as a filler is needed. Here is where the cucumber leaves come in handy. These leaves are easy to make and add another dimension to the arrangements.

1. To make the leaves, slice off the skin of the cucumber in a long strip.

2. Use the point of the knife and notch out the leaf as shown.

3. After the leaf has been notched out all around, use the point of the knife blade and "draw" the veins of the leaf. Place in ice water until ready to use.

See Color Plate 1

58

Cucumber Leaves

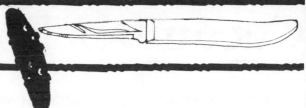

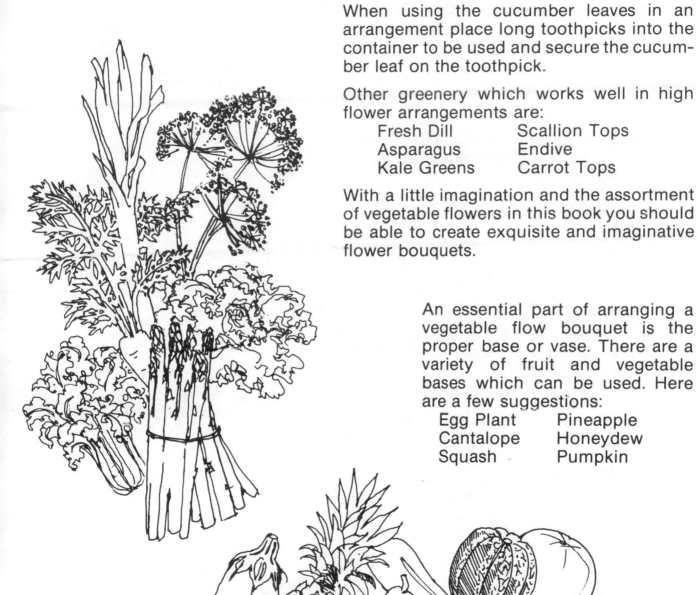

When using the cucumber leaves in an arrangement place long toothpicks into the container to be used and secure the cucumber leaf on the toothpick.

Other greenery which works well in high flower arrangements are:

Fresh Dill	Scallion Tops
Asparagus	Endive
Kale Greens	Carrot Tops

With a little imagination and the assortment of vegetable flowers in this book you should be able to create exquisite and imaginative flower bouquets.

An essential part of arranging a vegetable flow bouquet is the proper base or vase. There are a variety of fruit and vegetable bases which can be used. Here are a few suggestions:

Egg Plant	Pineapple
Cantalope	Honeydew
Squash	Pumpkin

Cucumber Rose

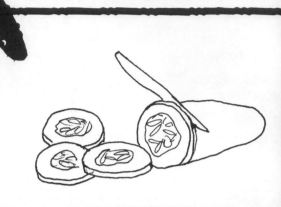

The cucumber rose is another variation of the sliced rose and one which is also very attractive when used as a garnish around a fish dinner or as part of a flower centerpiece.

1. To make this delicate flower, slice a cucumber into paper thin slices. Cut 5 or 6 slices for each rose.

Soak the slices in a salt water solution for 5 minutes. (1 tablespoon salt, 1 qt. water).

2. Use the smallest slice and roll it up tightly.

3. Take the next smallest slice and wrap it around the first rolled slice. From here on wrap each petal in the opposite direction as they are added to the flower.

4. Roll additional slices around each other, using the larger slices for the outside petals.

Secure the rolled slices with toothpicks. Use 2 or 3 toothpicks at the base of the rolled petals.

After securing the rolled petals with the toothpicks, gently fold down the outside petals and shape the rose.

60

See Color Plate 4

Cucumber Fish

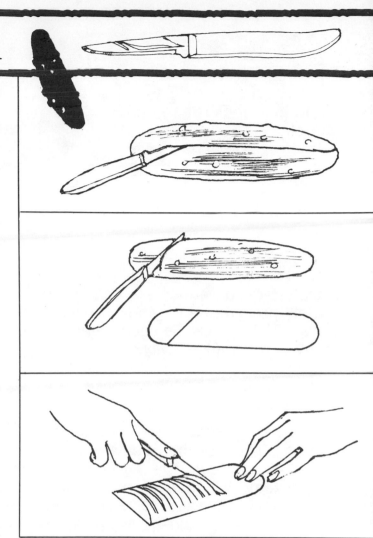

The cucumber flying fish is an ideal garnish to use whenever an extra touch is needed for a fish entré. This decorative garnish also makes an impressive decoration when it is used to accent a cold cut platter or a relish tray.

1. To make this decoration, slice a cucumber lengthwise into a long ½-inch thick slice.

2. Place this long slice with the flat side down and cut one end off at a sharp angle.

3. Start making diagonal cuts the full length of the cucumber skin following the same angle of the piece which was cut off. Be careful not to cut completely through the cucumber skin. Leave a spine when making these cuts to hold the slices together. Keep the cuts about ⅛-inch apart.

4. Soak the finished piece in salt water (1 tablespoon salt, 1 quart water) for 15 minutes to make the cucumber skin pliable enough to work with. When ready to make the flying fish, tuck under every other cut until you have 5 or 6 folded and place on platter.

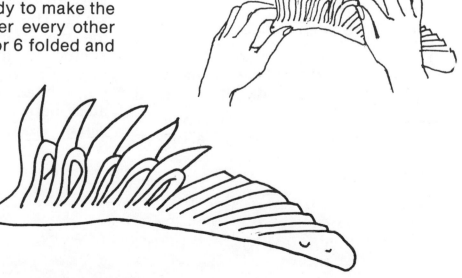

Egg Garnishes

Hard cooked eggs are basic to buffet presentations and appetizer trays. They can be decorated in many imaginative ways to create not only a pleasing garnish but they can also be prepared to make delicious eating.

The most important part of creating egg garnishes, or the popular deviled eggs, is to cook the eggs in the proper way. When eggs are cooked right they are easy to work with. If you follow these easy steps when hard cooking eggs you will have no problem in producing perfect cooked eggs.

1. Always start with eggs which are fresh and have been refrigerated.

2. If you are going to hard cook a large quantity of eggs, place them in a big pot, add water, salt and boil.

3. As soon as the water starts to boil violently, turn the heat down to allow the eggs to simmer slowly.

4. Eggs will coagulate in approximately 10 minutes. The cooking time starts as soon as the water starts to boil. If the eggs are overcooked, the yolks will turn a green color. This is because the sulphur, which is a component of the yolk, will come to the surface of the yolk ball and turn it green.

5. This step is the most important to produce perfect hard cooked eggs. As soon as the 10 minute cooking time is up, carefully pour off the boiling water and immediately chill the cooked eggs in ice water. This is done to form a "steam jacket" between the shell and the coagulated egg white. This steam jacket will cause the membrane inside the eggs to adhere to the inside of the shell instead of sticking to the coagulated egg whites. If the eggs are chilled after cooking the membranes will slip off easily.

Egg Chicken

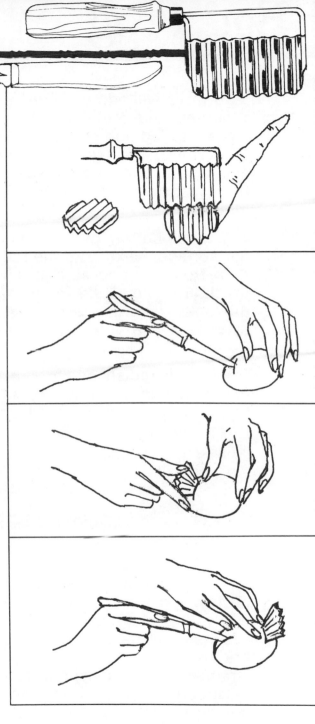

Another delightful garnish to place in and around a deviled egg platter is this chicken egg. The chicken eggs go over great at children's parties.

1. To make the chicken egg, cut off ⅛-inch slices of carrot using the garnishing knife. Cut these round slices in half.

2. Cut the egg to create a flat bottom. Use the point of the small knife to make a slit near the end of the egg. Insert the sliced carrot piece for the tail.

3. Make another slit to place another piece of carrot for the comb. Use small pieces of carrot for the beak and eyes.

STUFFED EGGS

Stuffed eggs can be used with, or as an alternative to, deviled eggs and used either way makes for delicious eating. Cut peeled, hard cooked eggs in half and remove the yolks. Place in the yolk chamber, either a smoked oyster, smoked salmon strips, caviar, minced lobster or pureed chicken liver and pipe on a border of egg yolk paste. Sprinkle with paprika or finely minced parsley.

Egg Frog

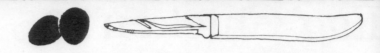

The egg frogs will add excitement to children's parties and a delightful touch to a deviled or stuffed egg platter.

1. To make the egg frog, peel a hard cooked egg and cut a pie-shaped wedge from just below the center to form the mouth.

2. Cut the bottom of the egg to create a flat surface. Next, take the red pimento strip from a pitted stuffed olive to use for the tongue. Cut 2 round slices from the olive to form the eyes. Attach the eyes with egg yolk paste (see Deviled Eggs).

3. Make a radish mushroom and turn upside down for the hat. Attach the hat with egg yolk paste. Place the egg frogs on lettuce, endive or parsley leaves.

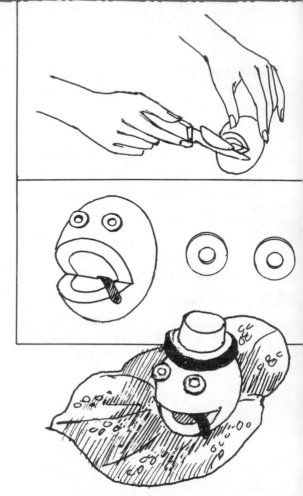

DEVILED EGGS

Egg yolk paste, also known as egg yolk cream, is used for most deviled egg preparations. To make egg yolk paste, mash 6 egg yolks (this is done best when the yolks are pushed through a sieve, or strainer.) Add ½ teaspoon salt, ⅛ teaspoon pepper, ½ teaspoon dry mustard, a small amount of lemon juice and enough mayonnaise, or heavy cream, to moisten (about 3 tablespoons). Whip mixture to a firm fluffy consistency. This mixture is very easy to apply on cooked egg whites when piped through a pastry bag with a decorative tip.

Refill egg whites creating decorative mounds of this seasoned yolk paste by squeezing the pastry bag.

NOTE: The egg yolk paste can be colored differently to give an eye appealing variety by blending tomato paste, pureed liver, pureed salmon or avocado paste to the mixture. Garnish the tops of the filled deviled eggs with small pieces of parsley, green pepper, pimento strips, thinly sliced carrots or olives by pressing these added garnishes into the egg yolk paste.

Fancy Fruit

The food decorator tool will do a beautiful and easy job of creating decorative edges on fruits and vegetables.

FANCY GRAPEFRUIT

That extra touch when serving grapefruit is made by pushing the point of the decorator tool into the center of the fruit. This will create a "V" cut. After you have made the first cut, make another cut directly next to the first one. Continue making these cuts around the grapefruit. After you have cut completely around the fruit, separate the two halves. Section the grapefruit and place a strawberry, cherry or grape on top.

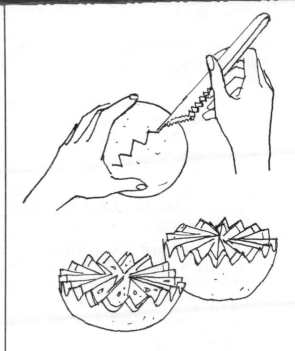

CANTALOPE ALA MODE

A delightful summertime treat is the cantalope ala mode. Cut the cantalope in the same fashion as the grapefruit. Scoop out the seeds using the other end of the decorator tool. Cut a flat surface on the bottom of the fruit. Place a scoop of ice cream in the center and top with a strawberry or cherry.

For a low calorie treat, substitute ice milk or sherbet for ice cream.

See Color Plate 3

Leek Flower

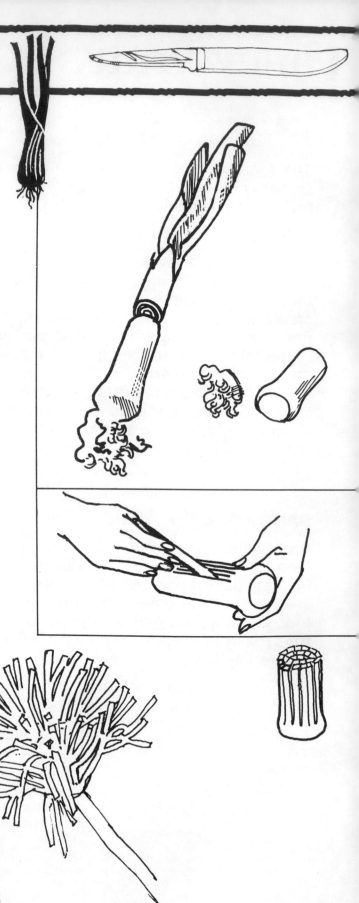

The leek onion makes a delicate and impressive flower for either garnishing or vegetable flower centerpieces.

1. To make the leek flower, select leeks which are about 1-inch in diameter at the base. Cut the roots off and wash the leek. Where the roots and layers of the vegetable meet there is a thick base like that on the bottom of a celery stalk. Slice through this thick base but do not cut it off completely.

2. Use the small sharp knife and make a downward cut from the root end of the vegetable. Make this cut straight down, cutting through all of the layers of the onion from the center of the onion.

3. Continue cutting around the outside of the leek until you have strips all around.

4. Put a toothpick into the end of the leek and twirl the vegetable to open the petals. Chill the flower in ice water for 5 minutes to open the petals further. To color the flower, put a few drops of food coloring into the ice water. This is the same type of flower as made from the scallion but larger in size.

Leek Ribbons

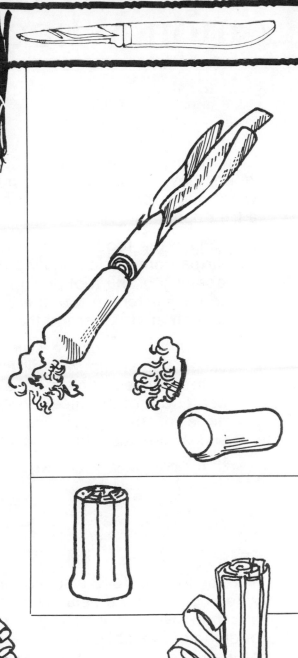

Another decorative touch for an appetizer or relish tray is the leek ribbon.

1. To make the ribbon, cut the onion as described under the leek flower. When slicing the vegetable around the outside, space the cuts further apart keeping the cuts about ¼-inch from each other.

2. Start with the outside layers of the cut leek and curve it around and tuck it in at the base of the onion.

3. After the bottom has been tucked in all around, take the second layer of the leek and continue tucking the layers in until you have reached the top.

To color the ribbon, place it in warm water to which a few drops of food coloring has been added. Let set for 5 minutes.

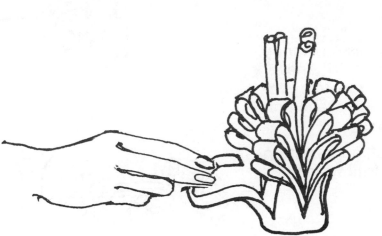

Lemon Wheels

Lemon wheels add a little decorative touch when they are used to top mixed drinks, watermelon basket handles, or floated in a fruit punch.

1. Use the food decorator tool and cut strips from the lemon by pulling the eye opening of the tool downward from the top of the lemon. Cut these strips about ½-inch apart all arond the fruit.

2. Cut the lemons crosswise into ¼-inch slices. If the lemon wheels are to be used to top a mixed drink, make a cut from the center out of the slice and secure on the edge of the glass. These decorative slices can also be used on most fish platters.

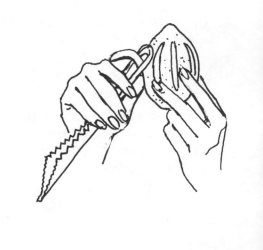

LEMON TWISTS
The decorator tool also comes in handy when cocktails are being served. Whenever a lemon twist is needed just run the eye-opening of the tool down the side of a lemon or lime and you have your twist.

NOTE: When using this tool on a lemon or lime, it is best to buy citrus fruit which has a thick skin.

Mushroom Garnishes

Mushroom garnishes are used for decoration as well as for food. Raw mushrooms to be carved must be firm and fresh. Care must be taken with mushrooms because they have a tendency to turn brown whenever they are cut or peeled, so rub them with lemon juice before cutting to keep them white. After they have been cut soak them in cold water to which lemon juice has been added. Mushrooms can be served raw, broiled, sauteed in butter, or baked in cream to create a delicious garnish.

STUFFED MUSHROOMS

Stuffed mushrooms are a delightful and appetizing treat and make a perfect appetizer or hors d'oeuvre. They can be stuffed with a variety of mixtures and kept at serving temperature by presenting them in a chafing dish. To prepare for stuffing, select large uniform mushrooms and remove the stems. Rub the mushroom caps with lemon juice and wipe them with a damp cloth. Put caps in lemon water and refrigerate until ready to stuff. Chop mushroom stems. Finely mince onion, parsley and chives and mix with chopped mushroom stems. Salt and pepper lightly. Saute chicken livers in 2 tablespoons butter for 2 minutes. Place sauteed chicken livers in a bowl and add a little tomato juice. Mash chicken livers and tomato juice until a paste consistency is obtained. Add minced onions, parsley, chives and chopped mushroom stems. Mix well and refrigerate until ready to serve. When ready to present, remove mushroom caps from lemon water and stuff with chicken liver mixture. Melt 3 tablespoons butter in a chafing dish. Add one chopped garlic clove to melting butter. Saute stuffed mushroom caps, stuffed side down, for 3 minutes. Carefully turn and continue to saute until brown all over. Serve as hors d'oeuvre or appetizer.

Mushrooms

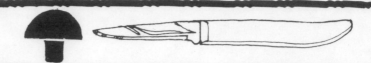

MUSHROOM FLUTED

To make this garnish, trim all but ½-inch of a large, well rounded mushroom. Hold the mushroom by the stem with one hand and with the other hand, cut little "V" (or wedge) cuts around the outside surface. Continue cutting these wedges to create a pin-wheel design.

Slightly turn the mushroom as you cut each wedge. Cut these small wedges from the center of the mushroom to the outside.

After you have created the pin-wheel design, press the tip (using the flat side) of the knife into the center to make the star design.

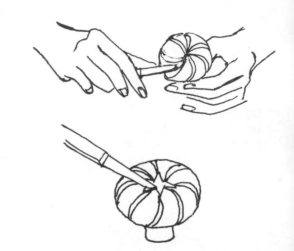

See Color Plate 10

MUSHROOM RELIEF

The mushroom relief is easier to make than it appears and is an impressive garnish when served with a fish dinner or placed with a cold salad.

1. Use the point of the knife (sharp edge) and draw the picture you want. The point of the knife should cut about ¼-inch into the crown when making the image.

2. After the image is outlined, trim about ⅛th of the mushroom crown. Be careful not to cut into your design.

To stay white, the relief should be kept in a solution of lemon-juice and water until ready to use.

To cook these mushroom decorations, place them in lightly salted boiling water for 3 minutes.

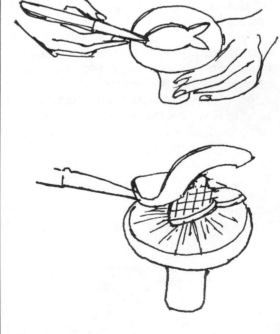

See Color Plate 10

Onion Garnishes

The onion also has a place in garnishing and when presented with the right background, offers a strikingly decorative garnish. Onion garnishes are usually not meant to be eaten but because of the delightful addition they contribute to meat and poultry platters, it is well worth the time to transform them into eye appealing garnishes.

Onion Mums

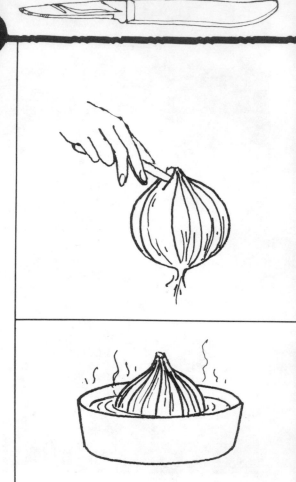

The onion mum looks like a lot of trouble to make, but it is one of the easiest garnishes to do. This garnish can be made in advance and can also be tinted to produce soft pastel colors for use in floral centerpieces.

Select a medium-sized, well rounded white onion. Choose onions which are uniformly tapered and avoid onions with a double growth inside.

Peel the outer skin of the vegetable. Leave the root end intact but cut off any roots.

1. Use the small sharp knife and starting at the top of the onion, make a cut downward towards the root end. Be careful not to go all the way to the root end but stop the cut about ½-inch from it. Make this cut deep into the center of the vegetable. Make a second cut in the same way and continue making these cuts until you have gone completely around the onion.

2. When you have completed cutting around the outside, place the onion in a bowl of hot water. This will start the petals spreading and remove the onion acid smell. Let soak for 5 minutes then replace the hot water with ice water to allow the flower to bloom further.

3. To color the onion mum, place food coloring in the ice water and let soak until the desired tint is obtained.

See Color Plate 5

72

Onion Cup

 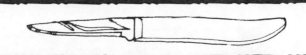

Onion cups add an appetizing extra touch to serving vegetables, and also an easy way to control portions when used in a buffet.

To make this easy and useful garnish, use large, well tapered onions. Peel the outside skin and saute in ½ cup butter over a low heat until tender but still firm (about 10 minutes). Remove and drain.

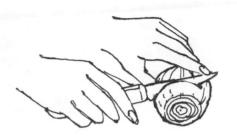

1. When cooled, cut the onions in half.

2. Carefully remove the inside section leaving ½-inch of the outside shell.

3. When ready to serve, fill these cups with cooked vegetables such as green peas, carrots, spinach, etc. The center layers of the cooked onion, which was scooped out, can be minced or chopped and mixed with other vegetables before filling the cups.

Orange Garnishes

Oranges are available most of the year and always offer a pleasing garnish when served with mixed drinks, as an individual dessert or combined with other fruit in a fruit salad. The orange is easy to work with and when in season is an inexpensive garnish which is always good eating. Most of the garnishes that are made from the orange can also be made with lemons, limes and grapefruit.

Orange Basket

Orange baskets give that professional touch to classic dishes, appetizer and relish trays. It is also a delightful garnish when filled with melon balls and fruit salad.

1. To make the basket, use a thick skinned or navel orange. With the decorator tool, cut strips using the eye-opening end of the tool, from the top (blossom end) of the orange to the bottom (stem end).

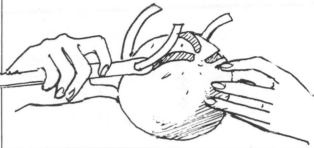

Cut these strips around the orange being careful not to cut the strips off. Cut these strips from the top to about ½-inch from the bottom. It is easiest to cut these strips when you follow the contour of the fruit.

2. Cut away wedges on both sides of the fruit so you are left with a "handle" in the middle of the basket. If the basket is to be filled, remove the orange pulp and trim around the handle.

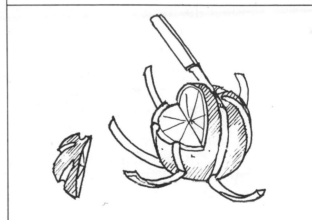

3. Fold the strips over and onto themselves to make loops all around the orange. Fill the area underneath the handle with watercress or parsley to simulate a basket. Refrigerate until ready to serve.

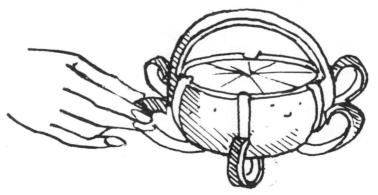

See Color Plate 10

Orange Elephants

The orange elephant becomes a delightful surprise when present at children's parties. A centerpiece of circus elephants can be made by using lemons, oranges and grapefruits to create different size elephants.

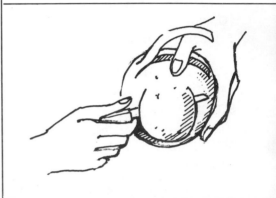

1. To make this fruit garnish, select a thin-skinned orange and with the small knife cut a large "Y" shape at the blossom end of the fruit, as shown.

Use the tip of the knife and carefully separate the skin from the meat of the orange. This will be the trunk of the elephant garnish.

2. Next, make a cut as if you were going to take a slice from each side of the orange. Do not cut all the way through the slice. These two slices will be the ears of the elephant. After the ears have been cut, gently pull the slices away from the body. Be careful not to pull too far or the ear might break off.

3. The tail is made by cutting a small "V" cut just above the stem end. Use the tip of the knife and raise this "V" cut slightly.

4. For the feet, use small marshmallows or gum drops, and secure them in place with toothpicks. For the eyes, cut a maraschino cherry in half; secure each half with a toothpick. Keep chilled until ready to use.

See Back Cover

76

Orange Surprise

The orange surprise goes over very well when used as a dessert. They are easy enough to make and can be made well in advance for any buffet spread or children's parties. To make this delightful treat use a firm thick skinned orange, of the naval type, with good color.

1. Use a small sharp knife and starting at the blossom end of the fruit make a cut from the top to, but not through, the stem end of the orange. Make the cuts deep enough to slice through the thick skin but not into the meat of the fruit.

2. Space the cuts evenly, starting at the top each time and cutting downward to form petals which are about ½-inch wide at the center. Be careful not to cut too close to the stem end.

3. When all cuts are made, carefully separate the skin from the meat of the fruit. Peel each petal separately until all petals are away from the body of the orange.

4. Gently twist the peeled orange meat away from the cut skin. If the skin was cut right it should remain in one piece when the orange sections are removed from it.

Use an ice cream scoop and fill the orange skin with either orange, lemon or lime sherbet. Form the sherbet into the same shape and size as that of the orange itself. Carefully close the cut petals around the frozen dessert one by one and press each petal against the sherbet so they will stay closed. Shape the orange skin to look as if it had not been cut. Place the finished orange surprise in a freezer until ready to be served.

77

Orange Cup

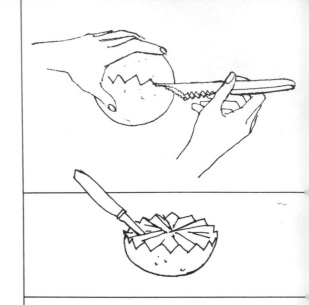

The orange cup is an impressive and useful garnish for Holiday spreads or whenever turkey is the main dish served.

To make these cups, use the decorator tool and cut the orange in half (see Fancy Fruits).

Take out the orange pulp being careful not to break the shell.

Mix the pulp with cranberry sauce and re-fill each orange cup with the orange-cranberry mixture. Place one of these cups by each place setting when ready to serve.

ORANGE GELATIN WEDGE

Another unique orange garnish for decorating or for use as a dessert treat at children's parties is the orange gelatin wedge. These wedges are especially attractive when different colors and flavors are used. When serving fish, use lemon gelatin; for lobster, cherry; for pork, mint.

To make the wedges, cut an orange or lemon in half with the small knife and scoop out the pulp being careful not to break the skin.

Refill the empty skins with hot, flavored gelatin and allow to set overnight. After the gelatin has set, cut the fruit cups into ½-inch wedges. Run the blade under hot water before cutting the wedges to make slicing easier.

Pepper Flower

The pepper flower is made from a red bell pepper and is known as an Anthurium. With the help of florist sticks, you can make a beautiful vegetable flower arrangement to use as a centerpiece (see Cucumber leaves).

1. To make the flower, cut the pepper into a heart-shaped design. Use the natural curves from the top of the pepper for the top part of the heart. You should get 3 or 4 hearts from 1 pepper. Place the hearts in cold water for 5-minutes to curl.

2. Next, shape a white radish, or turnip, into a round, pencil thin length about 1-inch long. Place in cold water to curl.

Sharpen the florist stick to a point, slide a green onion (scallion) leaf over the stick to hide it. Place the pepper flower on the point of the stick. Attach the radish, or turnip, stamen. Mix with scallion flowers, beet sliced roses and greens for a beautiful vegetable flower arrangement.

PEPPERS STUFFED

To add a decorative touch to stuffed peppers, use the decorator tool and cut the top section of the peppers (see Tomatoes Stuffed).

Scoop out the seeds and membrane of the peppers.

Parboil peppers in 1 cup lightly salted water for 5-minutes. Drain well and place on greased shallow baking pan.

Recipe
6 green peppers
1 lb. ground beef
1 cup cooked rice
1 cup tomato sauce
1 onion (diced)
1 tsp. salt
dash pepper
dash garlic powder

Brown beef and onions. Drain off fat. Add the seasonings, rice and tomato sauce. Mix together and continue to cook for 5 minutes over medium heat. Lightly stuff each pepper with meat filling mixture. Bake at 350° for 45-minutes. Serves 6.

See Color Plate 7

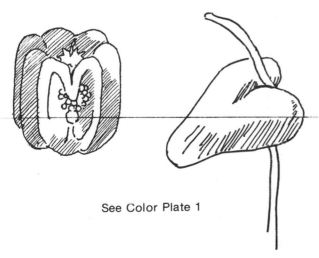

See Color Plate 1

79

Pickles

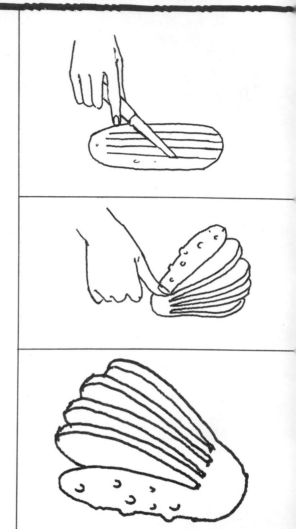

PICKLE FANS

1. Select a fat gherkin about 3 inches long. With the blade of the small sharp knife, slice the pickle lengthwise to but not all the way through the other end. Stop the cut about ½-inch from the end. Make 3 or 4 more thin slices in the same way.

2. Place the sliced gherkin on a cutting surface and with your thumb gently press on the end which is holding all of the slices together. This will spread the cut slices to form a fan.

3. These pickle fans can be placed on a sandwich plate, in a relish tray or on top of a meat loaf or ham to give it that finished look.

PICKLE ACCORDIONS

This is another of the popular pickle garnishes. To make the pickle accordions, select a fat, well rounded gherkin and cut off the tips of both ends. Lay the pickle on a cutting surface and make a series of evenly spaced cross-cuts, cutting into but not all the way through the gherkin. Hold the ends of the pickle and bend it gently into an arch to separate the slices at the top. Use this garnish on a sandwich plate or in a relish tray.

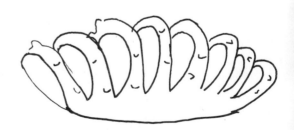

Potato Garnishes

Potatoes offer a garnish which is not only delightful to look at but also delicious to munch on. Even though raw potatoes are edible, raw potato garnishes are not practical to use because the starch in the vegetable turns a dark, unappetizing color in a very short time. This problem is solved by cooking the vegetable as soon as the garnish is created.

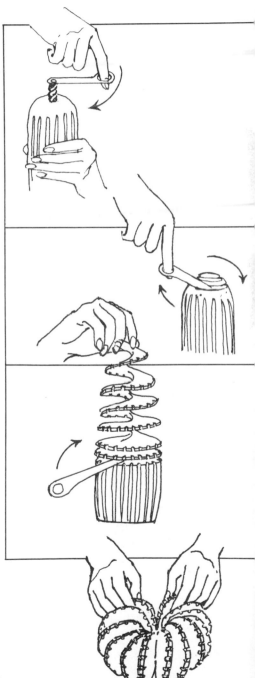

POTATO SPIRAL

1. Insert the screw of the tool into a potato so that the screw is in about half way. Place your index finger into the hole and rotate the tool clockwise.

2. The screw will work its way through the vegetable and at the same time the blade of the tool will slice a spiral design from the vegetable.

3. Once the spiral ribbon has been made, the two ends of the ribbon can be attached with a toothpick and the ribbon can be deep fried to make a decorative treat.

POTATO CHIPS

1. To make potato chips, home fries or cottage fries from the spiral ribbon, simply place the blade of a small knife down into the screw hole and make a single cut outward. Separate the slices and deep fry or pan fry to a golden brown.

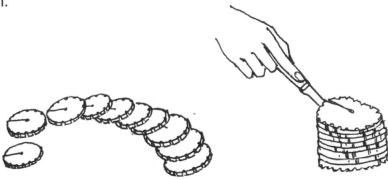

Potato Rose

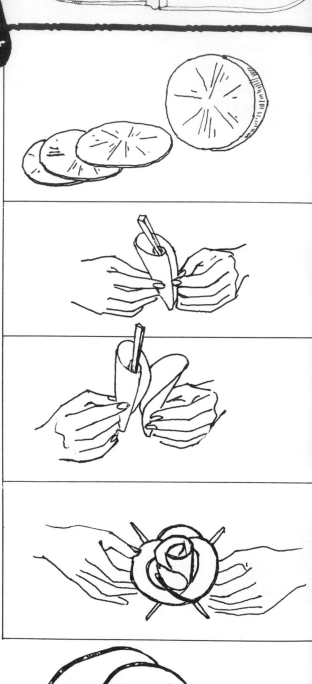

The potato rose requires more care in making than the other vegetable flowers but the effort put into mastering this flower will be well worth the time. To make this impressive flower wash and cut one large unpeeled potato crosswise into paper thin slices. Do the same with a second potato.

1. Using a carrot stick as the center, tightly roll one of the small thin potato slices around this carrot stick.

2. Wrap a second small slice around the first rolled slice, wrapping it in the opposite direction of the first slice. Add this second slice so it is rolled tightly at the base but spread loosely at the top. Add the next slice by placing it across, or opposite, the second petal. Hold these petals in place with a toothpick.

3. Continue adding slices using the larger potato slices for the outside row of petals and securing with toothpicks. Using 3 or 4 small slices for the inside petals and 3 or 4 large slices for the outer petals will create a nicely formed flower.

When finished shaping the potato rose, place the entire vegetable in cold water for about 5 minutes. Drain well and carefully deep fry the vegetable flower. After frying, allow the flower to cool, then gently remove all toothpicks and the carrot stick. The frying process will hold the petals together. When ready to display, place the potato rose on a bed of fresh parsley and arrange around any meat, game or fish entree.

Potato Stuffed

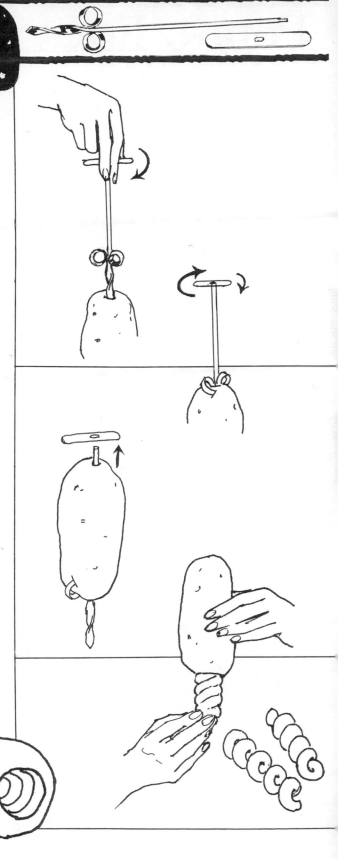

1. Attach the handle, use a light pressure and twist the tool into the end of the potato. Continue turning the tool as it works its way through the vegetable.

2. When the tool starts to come through the other end of the vegetable, detach the handle and pull the tool out of the potato completely.

3. Using your fingers, "TURN" the cut curls out by slowly turning counter-clockwise. Separate the two cut vegetable curls by twisting one curl out of the other. Deep fry for fancy potatoes.

STUFFED POTATO RECIPE

After using the twin curl cutter on potatoes, the hollowed potatoes remaining can be filled with seasoned meats or cheese to create a novel and delicious filled baked potato.

    6 medium-sized potatoes
    1 pound ground beef
    1 cup soft bread crumbs
    1 tablespoon chopped parsley
    1 tablespoon chopped onion
    1 teaspoon salt
    ⅛ teaspoon garlic salt
    2 tablespoons melted butter
    1 teaspoon paprika

Heat oven to 375° F. (moderate) Boil potatoes with the skins on for 15 minutes. Drain and pare. Saute the ground beef until brown and crumbly. Add bread crumbs, parsley, onion, salt, and garlic salt. Mix well and stuff into the potatoes. Place the stuffed potatoes in a shallow greased casserole. Brush with butter mixed with paprika and bake in oven at 375° F. for 25 to 30 minutes, basting with more butter if necessary, until tender.

Potato Fries

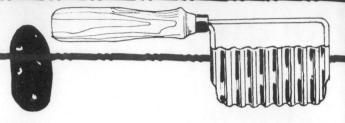

SCALLOPED DESIGNS

After washing and peeling a potato, simply use the garnishing knife around the outside of the vegetable to create a scalloped design. Next, slice the vegetable crosswise to make potato chips, cottage fries or home fries. This can also be done with carrots, beets, cucumbers or turnips to add that something extra to tossed salads.

KRINKLE CUTS

To make "krinkle cut" french fries, slice the potato crosswise into ½-inch slices. Place the cut slices flat on a cutting surface and cut the slices again in the other direction. Fry to a golden brown and serve.

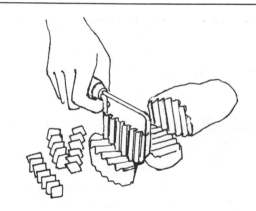

POTATO WAFFLES

Slice the vegetable crosswise in one direction, keeping the slice as thin as possible. After making the first slice, give the potato a half turn and cut off another thin slice. Continue turning each time a slice is taken off. Fry to a golden brown and serve.

Radish Garnishes

The radish is the most common garnish used and is very appealing. Radishes are obtainable during most of the year. When selecting radishes, choose the ones which are medium-sized for full flavor and best color. I have found that the very large radishes may look good but they are usually dry inside and are not very easy to work with when using them for garnishing. The best radishes to use for garnishing are the ones sold in bunches, with the green leaves still attached.

Radishes, as a garnish, can be used in many ways: they can be placed on top of a salad or displayed on parsley or watercress around most meat platters or as appetizers in a relish tray to be munched on by themselves.

RADISH WHIRLAROUND

Another novel and delightful garnish for a relish tray, sandwich plate or an eye appealing decoration around any meat entree is the radish whirlarounds. They are easy enough to make and will always get compliments when used as a garnish. To make the radish whirlarounds, select a medium-sized, well rounded red skin radish. Wash in cold water and cut the root tail and the stem end flat so that the radish will set upright on the flat surface.

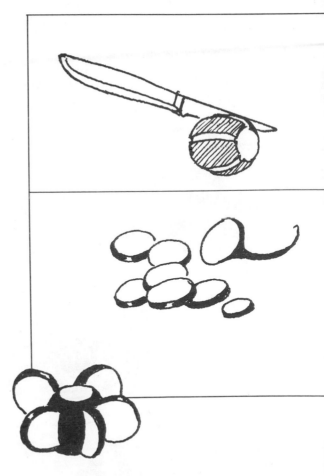

See Color Plate 8

1. With the blade of a small sharp knife, cut five evenly spaced "V" notches vertically around the outside of the radish.

2. Take a second radish and crosscut it into thin slices about ⅛th inch thick.

3. Select five evenly cut slices from the second radish and insert them into the "V" notches of the first radish. Place the finished whirlarounds in cold water and refrigerate until ready to use.

Radish Pompon

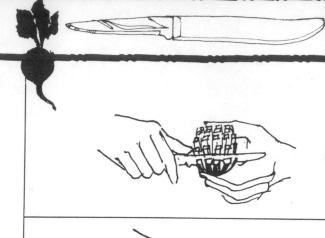

1. Select a well rounded radish and wash in cold water. Cut off the tail root and stem. Make a row of parallel cuts starting at the root end of the radish and slice to, but not through, the stem end. Keep the slices straight and close together.

2. After you have sliced the radish in one direction, give it a quarter turn and make a second series of cuts across the first cuts (forming right angles).

3. Place the cut radish in ice water and the petals will open into a puffy flower-like ball resembling a small pompon. Arrange the vegetable pompons on the salad plate and serve.

See Color Plate 8

RADISH ACCORDION

1. Select a long oval-shaped radish and remove the tail root and the stem. With the blade of a small knife, make a series of crosscuts into (but not all the way through) the radish. Space the slices close together and as evenly as possible.

2. After slicing, place the radish in ice water to force it open into an accordion shape.

Radish Spray

The radish spray is made from a long white radish and holds its own beautifully in any vegetable flower arrangement. This bloom can also be colored to make a mixed bouquet, which is very impressive.

1. To make this flower, select a well-tapered white radish. Hold the vegetable with the stem end toward you. Use the small knife and make thin slices from the root end to (but not through) the stem end.

2. Hold the lengthwise strips together and give the radish a quarter turn. Cut another series of lengthwise strips across the first cuts.

3. Place the cut radish in ice water for 5 minutes to bloom. To color this bloom add a few drops of food coloring to the ice water.

Radish Mouse

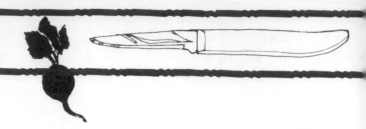

The radish mouse is a novel decoration to place in appetizer cheese trays. They are very easy to make and never fail to get a smile. Select one large oval shaped radish (with the root attached) and one small round radish (cut root off).

1. Cut 2 slices from a third radish to use for the ears.

2. Push a toothpick halfway into the large radish from the stem end. Slice 2 "V" notches in the small radish and place 2 radish slices in the "V" cuts for the ears. Make the eyes by pushing 2 whole cloves into the radish. Attach the small radish to the large one with the toothpick.

3. Position the head (small radish) on the toothpick protruding from the large radish. Complete the mouse using toothpicks for whiskers.

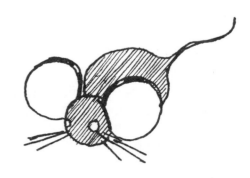

RADISH MUSHROOM

The radish mushroom is another clever decoration and an easy one to make.

1. Select a large, well-rounded radish and make ¼-inch deep cuts around the outside. Be careful not to cut too deep into the center.

2. Peel off ¼-inch of the skin (from the cut line down) to form the mushroom stem.

3. Use the point of the knife to make small white spots on the mushroom cap. Chill until ready to use.

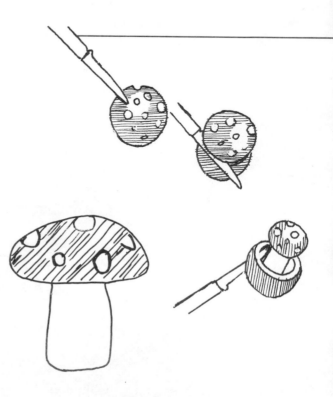

Radish Rose

 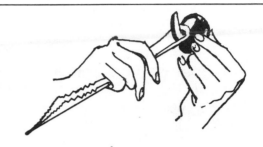

The food decorator tool in this kit comes in very handy for making the radish roses. Select a well rounded, or oval shaped radish, one with no splits in the skin.

1. Start making the first petal of the radish rose by placing the eye-opening end of the tool flat against the top, or root end, of the radish. Applying a moderate pressure, pull the decorator tool downward following the contour of the radish. Do not go all the way down, stop about ¼-inch from the bottom of the vegetable.

2. Repeat this procedure, keeping the cuts evenly spaced, until you have no more room around the radish for petals. After all the petals have been cut, use a small knife and remove the root tail.

3. If the radish rose is placed in ice water the petals will fan out even farther during chilling. The radish roses can be kept in cold water and will remain fresh and crisp for up to three days. The water should be changed at least once a day to insure freshness.

RADISH DAISY

The radish daisy makes a nice display in relish trays and vegetable flower displays.

1. Slice a well-rounded radish to get 5 or 6 petals. Take another radish and cut a flat surface at the stem end.

2. Cut 5 or 6 "V" notches around the outside of the vegetable and insert the radish slices to form the daisy.

Scallion Flower

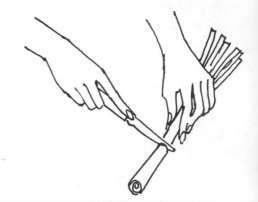

A delicate and impressive vegetable flower, which can be colored and arranged in many different ways to create an exquisite center-piece, is the scallion flower.

1. To make this flower, select scallion onions which are at least ½-inch thick at the base. Wash and cut off the roots but leave the root end intact.

2. Slice 2-inches off the root end.

3. Hold the scallion and, with the point of the small knife, cut into the center of the onion and make a slice out. Continue making these cuts all around the outside of the onion. Keep the cuts as close as possible.

4. Place a toothpick into the root end and give the vegetable a quick twist to open the flower. Soak in ice water for 5 minutes to curl. To color, put a few drops of food coloring into the water.

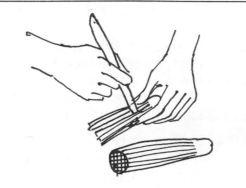

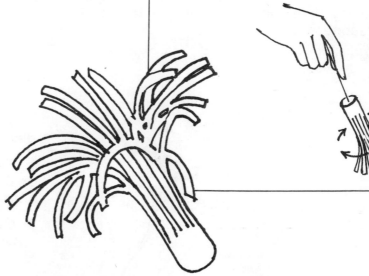

See Color Plates 1, 4, 9

90

Tomato Garnishes

Tomato garnishes are a must for most buffet spreads and an added delight when used as individual salads. The many ways tomatoes can be used makes them a most versatile vegetable for garnishing. The tomato garnish adds the right texture and color contrast to the green leafy vegetables used in salads.

They not only add a new dimension to the food being presented but they can also be used as a natural package which can be stuffed with a number of savory mixtures. The stuffed tomato salad will offer an easy way to control the right number of portions when setting up a buffet.

Stuffed Tomatoes

1. Select medium-sized, well rounded ripe tomatoes. Use the point of the Food Decorator tool and push this point into the center of the tomato. Make this cut by starting around the outside of the vegetable about 1-inch below the top, or stem end, of the tomato. Hold the Food Decorator tool so that when you push it into the vegetable and pull it back out, it will make a "V" shape. Place the Fancy Cutter point next to the "V" cut just made and push it into the vegetable again, creating a "W" shape.

2. Continue making these zigzag cuts all the way around the outside of the vegetable. Be sure to connect each new cut with the last cut made and keep the zigzag line as straight as possible. When the zigzag line is complete and you come around to where you started, the top of the vegetable will come off easily leaving a nicely trimmed tomato.

3. Use a small spoon and scoop out the pulp of the tomato to form a cup. Be careful not to break through the wall of the vegetable cup. It may be necessary to cut a thin slice from the bottom of the tomato to keep it steady when set on a plate.

4. After the zigzag tomato cups are hollowed, fill them with any salad mixture such as tuna, shrimp, egg, potato or salmon salad. After the cups are filled, sprinkle the salad filling with a little paprika and place the filled cups on a bed of lettuce. Top with a radish rose, stuffed carrot curl or the celery palm for a tempting and delightful salad.

See Color Plate 7

Tomato Wedge

Another variation of the stuffed tomato and one which comes in handy when mass production and time are essential is the spread wedge tomato. These can be made quickly and easily when a sharp knife and ice cream scoop are used.

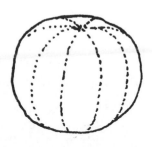

1. To make the spread wedge tomato, select medium-sized, well rounded ripe tomatoes. Cut the vegetable in half by starting at the top, or stem end of the tomato and cut to, but not through, the bottom of the vegetable. Stop the downward cut about ½-inch from the bottom end.

2. After the first downward cut has been made, give the tomato a quarter turn and make another cut in the same way across the first cut. Make two more cuts as if you were slicing a pie, dividing the tomato into eight evenly cut wedges which are still joined at the bottom.

3. When ready to use, spread the wedges open and with an ice cream scoop fill the centers with a mound of tuna, shrimp, egg, potato or salmon salad. Sprinkle a little paprika on top of the salad filling and place on a bed of watercress or lettuce. Top with a radish rose, stuffed carrot curl or the celery palm to add a finished touch to the spread wedge tomato.

See Color Plate 7

93

Tomato Strip Rose

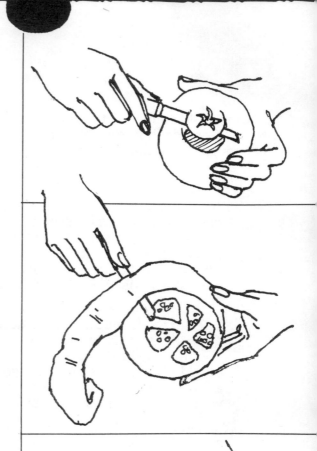

This vegetable rose is displayed best when it is placed around, or on top of, a meat entree such as a meat loaf, ham dinner or rib roast. Always place a sprig of parsley under this rose to complete the garnish.

1. Use the small knife and peel the skin of a medium-sized tomato. Start at the blossom end of the vegetable and cut a flat surface before continuing to peel the tomato. This flat surface acts as the base for the rose.

2. Keep the peeled skin as thin as possible and peel a strip about 4-inches long. Peel a second strip about 3-inches long.

3. Coil the first strip loosely around the flat base. Coil the second strip tightly and place it into the center of the loosely coiled strip. Shape the coiled peels into a rose in bloom.

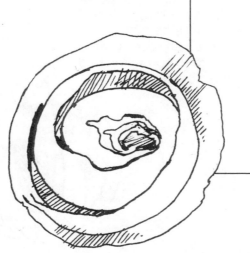

See Color Plates 1, 10

Turnip Lily

The turnip lily is an elegant looking garnish and makes a most striking centerpiece when mixed with other vegetable flowers. To make this centerpiece, shape a small piece of chicken wire into a dome and fill the spaces of the chicken wire by poking fresh parsley or watercress through these openings to create a mound of greenery. Arrange the vegetable flowers securing them to the chicken wire with toothpicks.

TURNIP LILY

1. Select a well rounded raw turnip of about 3″ in diameter. Wash and thinly peel the vegetable. Cut the turnip in half crosswise and cut off 4 thin slices. Make these slices as thin as possible.

2. Using the 1st thin slice, curve it into a cone shape. Hold this curved slice in one hand and with the other hand curve a 2nd slice around the first, wrapping it in the opposite direction of the first slice.

3. Secure the 2 curved slices at the base with a toothpick. Chill in ice water for a few minutes to set the shape.

4. Use a small strip of carrot for the stamen and place it inside the turnip lily. Make 4 of these lilies and place on the salad plate.

See Color Plate 12

TURNIP SNOWMAN

The turnip snowman is a delightful garnish for the winter holidays. It is also an easy one to make so let your imagination go.

1. Wash and peel three turnips, each one just a bit smaller than the other. Cut the largest of the turnips to create a flat surface. At the opposite end of the flat surface, push a toothpick halfway into this turnip.

2. Create another flat surface on the middle size turnip and secure this turnip on the toothpick protruding from the large turnip. Do the same with the smallest turnip, securing it with another toothpick.

3. Push whole cloves into the turnips for eyes, nose and buttons. For the hat, cut a thin slice from the thick part of a carrot and another thick slice from the tip of the carrot. Attach these two slices together with a toothpick and secure them to the snowman's head with another toothpick. Use a strip of pimento or scallion leaf (parboiled) for the scarf.

95

WATERMELON GARNISHES

When watermelons are in season they are a low cost source of fruit and can be carved into eye-catching centerpieces. Large watermelon basket are the most common of the centerpieces used for buffets but the watermelon can also be carved into several different designs such as a viking ship, a whale, or a handy and attractive punch bowl.

When choosing a watermelon to be used as a centerpiece or punch bowl, select one which conforms in size and shape with the item to be carved.

The watermelon should be fresh with a rich green rind and with no scars or bruises. The best way to test a watermelon for freshness is to find one, if possible, which still has a piece of vine attached at the stem end. Break a piece of the vine off; if it is dry and snaps off easily, the melon is ripe. If you are selecting a watermelon which will not be made into a centerpiece for several days then choose one which still has a moist green vine at the stem end.

Watermelon Basket

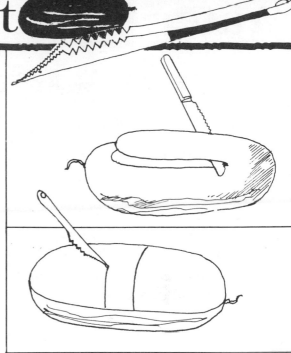

1. The watermelon basket is easy enough to make when using the Food Decorator tool. Select a well rounded, elongated ripe melon. Try to choose a watermelon which has a natural flat bottom or make a long bottom cut to prevent the centerpiece from tipping over.

2. When ready to make the basket, use the point of the Food Decorator tool and score (draw) the basket by making a horizontal line around the middle of the watermelon, dividing the melon into two equal halves. Next, score the handle by drawing two vertical lines (about 3-inches apart) across the center of the melon.

3. After the basket has been scored, start anywhere on the horizontal line, except between the two handle lines, and push tne point of the Fancy Cutter well into the melon. Keep in mind that the basket is made by cutting two large sections out of the watermelon, one on each side of the handle. Cut one side at a time being careful not to cut through the base of the handle. Make the zigzag cuts around the horizontal line until you come to the handle, then continue the cuts following the line.

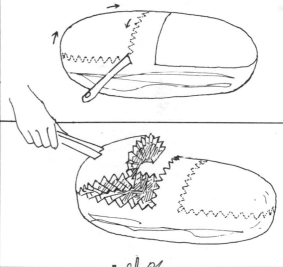

4. When the zigzag line is completely connected, push the point of the tool into the upper end of the watermelon and carefully lift the top section off. Repeat this same procedure on the other side of the handle and remove top section. Cut the red meat out from beneath the handle using a long sharp knife Follow the curve of the handle on the underside and cut away the red fruit close to the white rind. Continue to hollow the basket by removing the inside of the watermelon (a large french ball scoop or an ice cream scoop is handy for this job). Leave a shell about 1-inch thick by hollowing the melon close to, but not into, the white rind. Do not fill the basket until ready.

If the melon basket is carved a day or two in advance then wrap it tightly in transparent wrap and refrigerate until ready to use. When ready to fill remove wrap and fill with a mixture of "finger fruit" (finger fruit is any fruit which has been cut into bite size pieces). The watermelon basket can be filled with a variety of mixed fruit such as white and black grapes, blackberries, strawberries, cherries, cantaloupe balls along with the scooped out watermelon balls. To add a finishing touch to the fruit basket, cut an orange crosswise into ¼-inch slices and place them around the top of the handle, overlapping them slightly. Anchor the orange slices in place by pushing toothpicks through the center of the orange slice and into the rind of the handle. Leave about 1-inch of the toothpick sticking up through the orange and top the slices with a grape or a cherry.

97

See Color Plate 3

Watermelon Punch Bowl

The watermelon punch bowl is a tempting and attractive way to serve punch for any group gathering. Select a large elongated watermelon and follow the procedure for making the watermelon fruit basket with these two exceptions:

1. Instead of scoring the horizontal line around the middle of the melon, raise the line higher so the hollowed watermelon shell will hold more punch.

2. Cut off a thin slice from the bottom of the watermelon with a large knife to stabilize the punch bowl. Be careful not to cut too deeply into the rind.

When the shell is ready to be filled, add your favorite punch and ice cubes and float thin slices of oranges, lemons and limes. Decorate the base of the watermelon punch bowl with frosted grapes.

GELATIN OCEAN

Extend your creativity by setting the viking ship or watermelon whale on an ocean made of gelatin. Use a large serving tray or cookie sheet with a lip at least ¼" high. Dissolve the gelatin in hot water (green ocean-lime gelatin; blue ocean-unflavored gelatin with blue vegetable food color), pour into serving tray and refrigerate until set. When ready to use, set the watermelon centerpiece in the center of the tray. Line outside of tray with fresh parsley. To create a wavy effect on the "ocean", whip egg whites until stiff and fluffy; using a pastry brush, paint the waves on top of the set gelatin.

FROSTED GRAPES

If the watermelon basket is used as a centerpiece then surrounding the base of the melon with frosted grapes will add a decorative touch to the centerpiece. To make frosted grapes, combine slightly whipped egg whites with a small amount of water. Use a pastry brush and brush this mixture over clusters of washed grapes. While the egg white mixture is still wet, sprinkle the grape clusters with granulated or powdered sugar to create a frosted look.

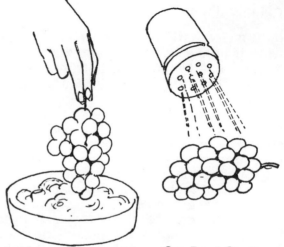

See Front Cover

Watermelon Whale

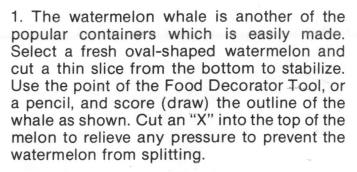

1. The watermelon whale is another of the popular containers which is easily made. Select a fresh oval-shaped watermelon and cut a thin slice from the bottom to stabilize. Use the point of the Food Decorator Tool, or a pencil, and score (draw) the outline of the whale as shown. Cut an "X" into the top of the melon to relieve any pressure to prevent the watermelon from splitting.

2. Follow the scored line making zig-zag cuts with the decorator tool. Cut a zig-zag pattern around everything except the tail and head. Use a medium-size knife to cut deep into the melon around the tail and head.

3. After cutting the pattern, do not attempt to take the top off in one piece. Instead, cut away small sections of the top to avoid breaking the tail section.

4. Carefully hollow the whale's shell with an ice cream scoop or large spoon. With the small knife, carve a big smile on the whale. Also cut two half moons for the eyes. Refill the watermelon whale with mixed fruit salad and set the whale on a gelatin ocean for a beautiful display (see gelatin ocean).

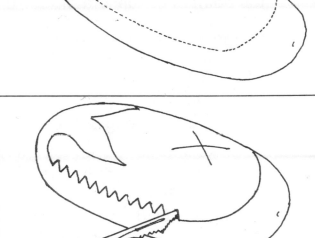

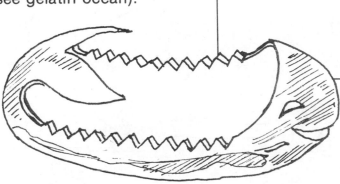

See Color Plate 2

99

Watermelon Buggy

The watermelon baby buggy is an ideal centerpiece for baby showers or birthdays for children.

1. To make this delightful design, use the point of the decorator tool, or a pencil and score (draw) the outline for the buggy as shown with the dotted lines. Use the decorator tool and cut a zig-zag line as shown.

2. For the carriage handle, use a knife and cut out the end section.

3. Make another deep cut down the center of the top and remove the two large pieces.

4. Scoop out the inside and mix with fruit salad. Carve the handle from the end piece. Place this piece with the green skin facing up and anchor it (use toothpicks if needed) into the end of the buggy.

5. For the wheels, slice an orange into ½-inch thick slices and secure with toothpicks. Refill with fruit when ready to serve.

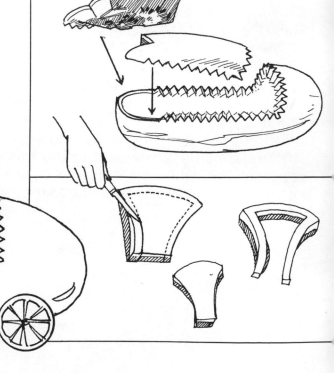

Watermelon Ship

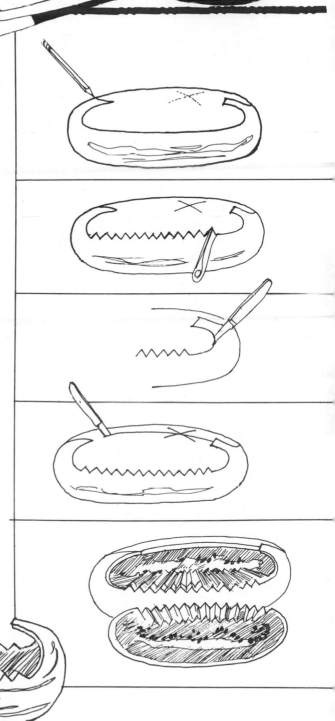

1. The watermelon viking ship is another novel way to present a fruit salad or a favorite punch. Select a long oval-shaped watermelon and stabilize the base by cutting a flat surface. Use the point of the decorator tool, or a pencil, and score (draw) the outline of the ship as shown. Cut an "X" into the top of the melon to relieve pressure to prevent splitting.

2. Use the decorator tool and make a zig-zag line along the sides of the melon.

3. With a medium size knife, cut deep into the melon, following the lines for the bow and stern of the ship.

4. Make a deep cut from the bow to the stern. Carefully remove one section of the top. Next, remove the other section. Scoop out the fruit to create the hull of the ship.

5. For an added touch, use the eye-opening end of the tool to create "plank" lines on the sides of the ship. Decorate the sides of the viking ship by making lemon, orange and lime wheels (see Lemon Wheels) for shields. Attach these shields with toothpicks sticking out and top the fruit slices with grapes, cherries, melon balls, etc. Use a sheet of poster board to create the sail and anchor it in the center with a long wooden dowel.

See Front Cover

101

Appetizers

Dips, canapes and tid-bits of food are popular appetizers which act as hors d'oeuvres at cocktail parties and first course servings at buffet parties. These appetizers are usually "finger food" and set the stage for an enjoyable party. The appetizers should require no spoons or forks for eating, and should be presented in such a way that they can be easily popped into the mouth. Appetizers should be "completely" edible. For cocktail and buffet parties, do not serve appetizers on clam shells, or food such as shrimp with the end tail attached, olives containing pits, etc. Keep your appetizers simple but with plenty of variety and color. Your appetizers should be of the tart, salty, crisp variety which go with drinks — nothing sweet.

The secret to good appetizers is simply — variety. Drinks are always standard so the food served with them should offer a variety of different colors, textures and tastes. The appetizers should be made so they can be eaten while sitting or standing without using utensils or plates, or finishing with sticky fingers.

The purpose of the appetizer trays is to keep the body and soul of the hungry guests together through the cocktail time, while allowing them to relax and move about the party freely. Appetizer trays of fresh vegetables, canapes, chips and dips should either be carried and offered to your guests or placed at different points in the room for easy picking. Be sure these trays are always replenished; a tray with only a few tid-bits on it always looks forlorn.

It is important to select and prepare as much food as you are going to serve, ahead of time. This is the secret for eliminating the scurrying, confusion and disappointment which usually happens when a party is not thought out or planned beforehand. PLAN AHEAD AND COOK AHEAD! Prepare as much and as many things as you possibly can a day or two before your party. Then on the day of your party, you can reserve your time in the kitchen to "assembling" your food, rather than spending your time cooking.

Canapes

CANAPES

As with dips, canapes give you a good head start in getting your party organized and your guests relaxed. Canapes also allow your guests to custom make their own open sandwiches with exactly the amount of spread they like. Your spreads and pates for the canapes can be made as much as a week beforehand, and in fact, will taste better if allowed time for the flavors to mellow and blend.

It is always best to place your sculptured spread in the center of a platter, or serving tray, and surround it with party sandwiches such as canapes which have a sampling of the spread as a topping. As the canapes are consumed, replenish the tray with an assortment of canape bread bases, or a variety of crackers. Planning your canapes this way will accomplish three things: 1) it turns the canape tray into a self-service appetizer tray;

2) any remaining spread will not have to be thrown away but can be refrigerated and used for sandwiches for weeks; and 3) the canape bread bases will not get soggy and limp.

CANAPE TOPPINGS

Select your toppings with eye-appeal by using the cream cheese and other white toppings for the dark bread bases and the more colorful toppings for the white breads. It is always best to serve the canapes soon after they are made; but if time does not allow this, you can spread the canapes a few hours before they are going to be served, and keep them fresh as follows: Cover a piece of stiff cardboard with waxed paper or plastic wrap. Place the finished canapes on the covered cardboard and cover them with a clean damp cloth. Store in a cool place.

Here Are A Couple Of My Favorites

Deviled Ham Topping:

1 6 ounce can deviled ham
3 ounces cream cheese, softened
1 teaspoon prepared mustard
           Yield: 3 cups
Mash deviled ham and softened cream cheese together. Blend in the prepared mustard.

Chopped Liver Topping:

1 cup ground, cooked chicken livers
1 6 ounce package cream cheese, softened
2 chopped hard-cooked eggs
2 tablespoons minced onion
  salt and pepper to taste
           Yield: 3 cups
Combine all ingredients and blend well. Cover and chill at least 1 hour before spreading on canape bread bases.

Bon Appétit!